Love and *Chaos*

Poetry and Lyrics in Motion

GIULIA RICCIARDI

Love and Chaos
Published 2019 by Your Book Angel
Copyright © Giulia Ricciardi

All rights reserved. No part of this book may be reproduced, stored, or transmitted by any means—whether auditory, graphic, mechanical, or electronic—without written permission of both publisher and author, except in the case of brief excerpts used in critical articles and reviews. Unauthorized reproduction of any part of this work is illegal and is punishable by law.

The characters are all mine, any similarities with other fictional or real persons/places are coincidental.

Printed in the United States
Edited by Keidi Keating
Layout by Rochelle Mensidor

ISBN: 978-1-7341814-1-8

Table of Contents

My Story ix
Just a Girl 1
My Twisted Ride 2
Cupid's Arrow 3
A Burning Rose 4
Satisfaction 5
Enchanted 6
Forbidden Love 7
Beast Within 8
A Reflection in the Mirror 9
A Captured Moment 10
Time 11
Lyrics on Canvas 12
A Valentine's Request 13
In Doubt 14
Me and You 15
Limited Passion 16
A Last Request 17
You 18
User 19
Curse 20
Obscured 21
Snapshots of You 22
Deep Inside 23
A Burning Ambition 24
For Love 25
Thief of Hearts 26
Mystic Me 27
Lost Love 28
Deceived 29
For Hurt 30
A Frail Heart 31
Spared Creation 32
Crossed by the Heart 33
Scents of Life 34
True Words 35
Reminisce 36
Alone 37
Drifted Off 38
Stoned Thoughts 39

Lost in a Dream	40
Alive	41
Embraced	42
Friendship	43
My Valentines	44
Elements of You	45
Path of Light	46
A Promised Land	47
Scattered Heart	48
Dissolved	49
Captured Soul from a Heart of Darkness	50
The Dominant vs The Unknown	51
Chaos of Love	52
Lost Fantasy	53
Torch on Fire	54
Awaiting the Mystic	55
Scattered Image	56
It's About….	57
Aiding the Mend	58
Scattered Thoughts	59
My Prayer	60
Black Raven	61
Poisoned	62
One in Darkness	63
Land of the Dead	64
Awakening Soul	65
Justice Laid	66
Complete	67
Signs of Affection	68
Stay	69
Note to Self	70
A Picture	72
The Visions I See	73
Linger	74
Confucius	75
Passive Bearing	76
A Hope and Prayer	77
I'm Still Waiting	78
It's Your Life	79
Gang War	80
Higher Learning	81
Surviving the Game	82
The Follower	83

Hope	84
True Forgiveness	85
Avail the Soul	86
Visual Thoughts	87
Scrambled	88
Sun Embraced	89
The Fighter	90
Shine	91
Forgive and Forget	92
Plantation of Pain	93
Elements of Life	94
Beyond Misery	95
Lost Compassion	96
Absence	97
Released	98
Images	99
A Wilderness Cry	100
Soldier Within	101
Exodus	102
Consumed	103
Departure	104
Denial of Love	105
Exhausted in Thought	106
Justified	107
Cast Away	108
Emptiness	109
Imperious	110
The Shining	111
The Watcher	112
Twin Soldiers	113
Memory Lane	114
Puzzled in Time	115
My Hero Envisioned	116
In Control	117
Unpredictable	118
No Strings Tonight	119
My Gladiator	120
Say Nothing	121
Implicated	122
Consumed in Fear	123
The Preacher	124
Can You Hear Me?	125
This Planet We Grow	126

Balanced	127
Coloured in Sin	128
Complicated	129
Fighting Battles	130
On My Own	132
A Feeling Repressed	133
Lost Boy	134
My Prayers to You	135
A Friendship Marked	136
As You Are	137
Faded	138
This Ghost	139
Suffocated	140
Voice of Reason	141
Changing the Game	142
Karma	143
Resolute	144
Crowned	145
Embraced Friendship by Valor	146
The Dance	147
Bitten, I Awoke	148
If I	149
My Path	151
Another Crush	152
Follow Me	154
The Player's Side	155
A Vision in Thought	156
Balancing the Times	157
Ring Me a Tune	158
Tripping Over You	159
I Hear from You	161
Common Mistakes	162
Hurting Inside	163
Letting Go	165
That Girl	166
Just an Adventure	167
Live Another Day	168
A Dream	169
The Secret Garden	170

`It takes a second for someone to say
Hurtful words and knock you down.
Just remember it takes that moment
To happen to inspire you and turn
Those words to a masterpiece.
Don't allow other's hate and
Misunderstanding consume you.
Know your worth.
-G.R.-

My Story

When I was young, I experienced a lot of different emotions due to loved ones, friends and young love. I felt alone at times as the only way to express myself was by listening to music and writing down my thoughts in lyric form. I remember I started writing lyrics as young as 14 years of age. That book is yet to be found as it's packed away. Then I watched a movie called Poetic Justice which inspired my writing to poetry. It calmed the storm inside me and made it easier to write in a flow that I could express and understand.

Sometimes it got dark and sometimes it was just a basic expression of what I visualized and experienced at that moment in time. It could have been where I was, who I was with and what I was doing at that time. Nonetheless, I always had a reason to write. I guess you could say it was my way of self-therapy as times were tough for my family and as a child to a teenager I got bullied and teased a lot in school and my surroundings.

There was also a period in my life which was tainted, and part of my childhood was tormented. Being raised in a strict family made me afraid to express what I was going through and feeling inside. It became a struggling battle of emotions. So, I placed all I felt on paper. It wasn't the greatest era of my life, I guess. We were not that well off, farmers and construction workers, children starting work at a young age, and it felt as though the community didn't like my family much. As a family we survived and pushed on through no matter the naysayers. It was a learning curve to say the least.

As I grew older, relationships were a bit hard for me to grasp and follow. They always ended up chaotic. Friendships... well, let's just say the naive always get torn by betrayal and I was always the one left to be shunned and alone. The only thing that allowed me to mentally stay stable was music and my writing. Throughout the years I shared my pieces with friends and had a few published by The National Library of Poetry and The Canadian Institute of Poetry. I had plaques made and printed as well. It was my passion. I even received an editor's choice award in 1997. I tried other outlets to branch out. I was unsuccessful. Though I took a break in trying I kept writing, always promising myself to try again when the time was right. Then again, I also said it would be my retirement when I decided to try and get published.

I took a ten-year hiatus from writing as things were good in my life. Let's be honest, it's kind of hard to write when you're happy. The best pieces of work come from deep within. For me, it was always chaos or deep emotional experiences that would get me going. Trust me, I tried to write when I was happy; those pieces weren't good enough. Then, while in my happiness, we hit a hard time and lost a child. Our little Angelica, born too soon. Then a close friend passed, then things just kept spiraling down for me. It was one thing after the next. So much hurt and people passing away. It was hard. I was fortunate having the man I love by my side through our drastic experiences. I couldn't imagine why he stayed but I guess there is real love after all. I started writing again and continued my journey. I chose to change my life and separate what was toxic in my life and I branched out in a different direction. Focusing on just us. Within that time, we were blessed with another child and I would write every now and then, but it was hard as time just couldn't permit me to do it. A lot was going on.

I always stated one day I would find someone who would be interested in my pieces and I would put myself out there to be heard. It took a hard lesson with friendships and moment in my life again that lit a fire under my ass to start typing away. I couldn't stop even if I tried. So, I put myself out there and reached out to social media outlets and Keidi Keating took an interest. I was shocked and excited and I couldn't believe in the past 25 years of writing my moment had arrived.

Now this first bit I share with you is just a peek into my life from a young girl to my adulthood. Follow the evolution into my writing, into my world. It's my story, my emotions, experiences, love and chaos I share with you. Maybe you can relate and connect with the poems. Take a moment and try to embrace those feelings as it will help you to understand what I'm unveiling to you, the reader. Until we meet again in Part 2 of my story. Enjoy.

Giulia Ricciardi

Just a Girl

I'm just a girl, whose words can be set hot like fire
It sets people off kilter, unleashes their deep desires
Sometimes it can be good, sometimes it can be bad
For some it makes them happy, sometimes just mad
I can't help myself for its who I am, no curtains to hide
I believe in free expressions, hell it's how I learn to survive

The best of people's heads can be in a wrong place
To hear the truth, to stand tall, to leave without a trace
I can be a tragic story or a beautiful disaster at best
I love too hard, give too much of my emotions just to test
It's not my given intentions to do wrong, create drama
Things seem to get twisted in turns to emotional trauma

What happens behind closed doors just releases a beast
Trouble just seems to find me, it's like a hungered feast
Not all seem to understand this driving force inside
Every decision I make at times I can be so blind
It's never planned out, I just seem to pick the wrong door
Shit, what the hell has this planned out, a thirst for more

So, I hurry up to make temporary decisions, it's my reality
Question every time "is this really my planned destiny?"
A word thrown, and a spark is set off in nature's way
Oh hell, what have I really done, it just burns my day
For I am just a girl, no one special, with just lots to say
If you don't like it, well, my advice, just keep away.

By: Giulia Ricciardi

My Twisted Ride

Crazy as it's seems a light has turned on
Comes a time for every story's dream to live on
We all have adventure, we all make believe
The real battle hurts, no matter the feed
And when we turn to face one another
We come to find just to uncover
The cursed truth is how it disguises
No truth behind what I thought I realized
No more games, no time to sit and wonder
The reality of it all becomes what I need to conquer

How do I separate the images I hold at stake?
These lyrics I speak, is it all my big mistake?
I only wish to share what I hold deep inside
It's all become so scrambled, waiting to collide
I carry for a moment, how I'm liberated
Locked in my mind, battles I can't separate
For if I fall for a second, I just can't deny
Another reason to protect what I can't disguise
The truth be given what the hell is this fight
In translation, I just want to scream inside

Can you feel the strain, can you step inside?
This battle that conquers with its deepest ties
Don't judge me wrong, hold on to the attack
I can see the weak, it's just what I seem to attract
For I come to realize we all have ghosts who ride
We fear the journey it takes towards darkened skies
We are sculped at best to become strong and fair
For no words of hate could amuse or compare
So, take a second and envision a place of salvation
Few and far between the twisted world of complication.

By: Giulia Ricciardi

Cupid's Arrow

Sculptures carved, portraits painted
Their shadows framed, bodies tainted
A shine enhanced with an envious reflection
An imaged grasped by its erection

Embrace my body as the rain purifies my soul
Like silk pearls that kiss the flesh of gold
Bliss is what I seek, left to find your treasure
I indulge for lust and passionate pleasure

You are the sculpture to what is carved
With a heart molded strong, slightly scarred
An image held high, full of pride
A hidden treasure painted in disguise

Velvet skies enhance images as they appear
Grasping each moment, I bleed coloured tears
Paint this portrait with each tear fallen
And you'll find a deeper meaning is calling

Cascades roar with power and grace
Protected from the wild, surrounding its place
Bestow on mountain's highest peak
Shall I climb, to embrace this sculpture I seek

In every stone and portrait painted lies an inscription
It defies its place with a given expression
For this I pledge is my gift to you
Engraved shall state: truly, madly, deeply you.

By: Giulia Ricciardi
February 1998

A Burning Rose

Her smile cracks in pain, this girl so beautiful
There she goes in the rain alone, it's crucial
As she dances alone, she sets off to soar
Yet inside her mind is that constant roar
Drowning in her sorrows, yet a painted picture
A rose that's tainted by others was once so pure
She's left her demise with the hidden intentions
As she neglects the lies reflected by its attractions

So visible, but not yet noticed
As she's burning the roses
Dying to be loved, she hides a scar
Her pain is deep, yet sets the bar
Desired for love, she carries on
Washing away her fears, she's gone

A harmonious light dying to be loved
Blinded this creature who is so beloved
A burning rose gone without a trace
Still breathing, she sets out to find her place
Sick with disappointment she hurries
Covered in tears, yet her smile endearing
Her eyes burning from the mascara running
Alone she may cry, this girl is still cunning

As she shapes her being, her wine embraces
As in time she set out, clearing the painted faces
Her heart has been broken many times, it's frustrating
This burning rose prevails herself without hesitating
The ashes will scale off and she will bloom once again
Leaving behind the dust from the rose burned in pain
Though tainted by others, her future a cover story
Awaits her time to stand tall, awaits in her glory.

By: Giulia Ricciardi
July 2007

Satisfaction

Pictures of you scatter through my mind
My heart starts to throb, so I confide
As the sweat starts to pour down, my body trembles in fear
Your presence surrounds me, this I can feel
As the image appears closer, you stand before me
As this becomes so clear, your body I can feel

I whisper softly to hold me close
As I press myself against you, become your host
As we touch, we become one in complete darkness
The night is clear, and we begin to express
Follow me into ecstasy I plead
And we will make love to its melody

Shhh, no words are spoken, not a word
Just close your eyes and let your body move
Can you feel it; our bodies heating
Can you hear it; our hearts beating
Move with me and I will hypnotize
My passion is burning to have you mesmerized

My lust is yearning, our bodies on fire
Satisfaction, this I assure you, a moment set for desire
Comfort your wounds, soften your touch, lasting our kiss
This a moment not to be missed
The sorrow hidden, the tears forbidden
Quench our desire, take on the heat
The passion that's burning sure can't be beat.

By: Giulia Ricciardi
July 29th 1993

Enchanted

In the enchanted land the petals will fall
With the dust of the wind, the melody shall sing
A voice so strong calms the land
As she waits upon the touch of his hand

With the willow trees and old oak twine
The sun's rays strong with the brightest shine
The sounds of chimes are so strong
Hoping the choices made won't be wrong

As she walks upon the path of stone
Her thoughts are deep, she holds her own
Someone to hold, someone to desire
Someone to share, someone to admire

At last the sun starts to go down
No love yet to find, she's left a frown
A lonely heart she wished to mend
A lonely night to her journey's end

She rests upon the willow's pasture
A peaceful soul, with a heart so pure
Weakness withholds her, hopeless in trying
A lonely soul with a heart that's dying.

By: Giulia Ricciardi
August 1994

Forbidden Love

Love is what hurts us so
A part of life which we all know
A part of life which most people cherish
Hurts to know all hearts get perished

To feel, to hope, like a fantasy
To suffer in pain is reality
A smooth lip, a bad attitude is what's given
No regrets, no rewards, no guilt hidden

To walk towards an endless game
For you are left to blame
To turn and curse upon his demand
A mistake, the dominate man

Try to understand my plea, my cry
Just to enter a hurtful lie
Your love is the ending
You must leave what's damaging

His intentions a grave, with a mind set free
His soul is cold, a heart of steel
A passion for all is wanted
This lover is nothing but haunted

A forbidden love is all you carry
Reflecting the pain is what you bury
Not wanting to be involved in such a mess
Time to move on, time to put this to rest.

By: Giulia Ricciardi
October 1994

Beast Within

Isolated in a world beyond these gates
Engaged with passions that curse the fate
Desired by the hunger of time
Controlled by the hidden cries

Shades of dark possess the mind
Colour of red glosses over the eyes
Vengeance grows within the heart
For the thirst of blood never parts

Like an animal, it lurks the nights
Destroying all in its path, all in sight
As the power excites the soul within
Darkness has taken it toll with sin

Alleviated inside all but its loneliness
The world its rendered has become hopeless
To release the hurt affected by its curse
Its feared by all its changing verse

The more it grows towards the dark
The thought of termination never parts
As this changing soul walks amid the fallen sky
Though it's damned, its determination is to survive.

By; Giulia Ricciardi
July 24 1995

A Reflection in the Mirror

Like flowers that turn to rain
An image deceived by pain
Though shadows seek and pray
A hurt that shall not lay

Like the cold that wraps the soul
Possessed by a fear has taken its tole
Though passive, yet confused in mind
A fact beneath the heart behind

A darkness behind solid walls
A trail behind the steps that fall
An image portrayed an illusion
A thought cursed beyond conclusion

Still a smog, a question to thought
Knowing nothing's inside the heart
Though followed and accepted
A confession never to be deceptive

Flesh and stone deep inside my soul
Captured beneath the darkened hole
Though never unleashed but kept hidden
A hatred kept beyond the forbidden.

By: Giulia Ricciardi
April 5 1996

A Captured Moment

Sometimes the wind carries without a noise
As the tide crashes and shatters its poise
Leaving the trees swaying to move in harmony
As the sky above changes its colour of destiny

As darkness hovers, the wild are awakened
Leaving its surroundings, tempers shaking
The dusk lays over the desolate grounds
For the wild run free to their destined bound

Then devil's night embraces the land
And the wicked hunt their prey in demand
The sea of night is still through dawn
The stars above dance while the wild spawn

Daybreak cracks and the fog lifted
The morning sounds, a melody drifted
Across the enchanted land the wilderness rises
It takes your breath, keeping you memorized

For the rays of night shine like gold
And the image withheld is cherished and told
A captured moment warming the heart
Calming the soul, regretting to part.

By: Giulia Ricciardi
July 28 1996

Time

Hands which melt as they drift about face
Movement that never sits, runs its pace
Disarmed, it embraces and dissolves
Depressing, it holds, yet faces evolve

Possess my thoughts of you, so spared
So beautiful, so passionate beyond compare
For a separation drifts and falls behind
An endless time freezes, powers its find

Time sits and melts our sorrows, bleed our heart
Why must it elapse and keep these arms apart?
Embracing, it feels, never known to release
Empowered, its thoughts left to bleed

It rhymes in circles, runs its pace
Chimes so sour, it creeps about face
I close my eyes and slowly drift along
Searching for the answers, my heart stands strong

In arms, feeling my embrace, capturing desire
Possess the mind, releasing its lust for fire
I reach and grasp your touch, embrace your heart
Connecting our bond that was so drifted apart

For each melting minute, each powered embrace
I release your mind, awaking our silence
Time, an essence, disarmed its own face
Possessed, I have you, envisioned in a sacred place.

By: Giulia Ricciardi
November 2 1998

Lyrics on Canvas

I reach for love, I receive its lust
I grasp to touch, I feel its dust
Releasing its care, embodied its pain
My heart I give, regrets, held in vain

Thoughts scatter and a picture I paint
For the image withheld bleeds and taints
I carry on a path and reach for direction
Followed within and found an infection

Absorbed, I've become spelled to my fold
Its visions turn, becoming pure as gold
For memorized, my soul becomes drifted
The pain enhanced weakens, becomes lifted

Picture an image, overtake the dare
The damage done becomes spared
For a wickedness withheld my grasp
A tenderness I seek becomes the task

A puzzle has turned to a game never-ending
Visions painted on canvas turn descending
Such words unleashed carve into lyrics
Its form preached detains its relic

You've turned dry like the hands of time
The virtue of patience has embodied the tides
For I shall enhance visions revealed
The canvas painted empowers life's melody.

By: Giulia Ricciardi
April 15 1999

A Valentine's Request

When I first met you, you made my life complete
But you felt so far, warm and sweet
All it took was one glance,
I thought, how could I get the chance
Afraid, I feared you would reject
So, I kept my distance, never to forget

As time went by my feelings grew stronger
For I couldn't hold back much longer
But I couldn't find the right words to say
To express why I felt this way

But I must open my heart, for I am strong
For I've kept it hidden far too long
I understand if you do not accept
Just promise me you will not forget

I would like you here to hold you tight
To love, to hold and cherish the nights
To give my trust under the stars so bright
Will you give me the chance to be in your life?

Just take some time and look deep inside
Look in your heart and you will find
A sacred love that will never die
The chance to take here is a leap in time.

By: Giulia Ricciardi
February 12, 1994

In Doubt

Now, my love, what must it be
That has attracted you to me
Unsure and in doubt, I have in place
For the sweetness of your face

A forsaken love you have unleashed
The forbidden cries you've put to peace
A feeling of being empowered
A force within you have uncovered

You've broken the chains of a lonely heart
Now it's set for a new start
You've captured its soul, given it life
Brighten up such darkened nights

But for this I must confide
A showered doubt still ponders my mind
A feeling I can't shake free
The fear of you loving me

I haven't had the best fortune in life
Its always been full of strife
My desire not to create pressure
To ensure what is measured.

By: Giulia Ricciardi
March 10, 1994

Me and You

I have an inspiration which guides me to
Feeling this expression, so I reach to you
Seems so crazy to even dream
A lot of time just left in disbelief

Time is short, and I'm left to contemplate
It doesn't matter, I just seem to hesitate
I can separate it, or try to forget about it
This picture feed aims to be a perfect fit

Drifting away, I do this at the best of times
Only a checking point, not to cross the line
Somehow, somewhere we got lost in time
Mistakes are made as if it was a crime

We have a timeline of our written past
Funny how it seems it's made to last
Carry on our differences, yes, we do
Only to find in the end, it's just me and you

I sacrifice and throw it all away
Forget its drama and blow it astray
For each time I turn I can see your face
Then again, I just thirst for your taste

So, I drift and disappear in your eyes
Follow its examples and believe in your lies
Knowing what you foresee in disguise
The hurt you have caused is no prize.

By: Giulia Ricciardi
June 2004

Limited Passion

Like broken glass that reflects the light
The mirror's reflection shattered night
Driven by compressed emotions
Separated by human devotion

In doubt by the love carried
Embraced by the emotion buried
Fooled by its sensitivity
Blindsided by its reality

The streets of crowded herds
The lyrics of shattered words
Lost in the forgiven stage
Mesmerized in the hidden rage

The forgotten to the given
For the part in shame hidden
The quarter mile left at stake
The journey ahead to my sweet escape

A forbidden lust which creeps inside
The punishment laid I cannot confide
A frame of mind lost in pursuit of betrayal
A desire wanted, yet caused an upheaval

Hypnotized by a glance
Forgotten by the given chance
A passion left to burn the soul
Which mends the heart wanting more?

By: Giulia Ricciardi
March 1 1996

A Last Request

You may not understand the life I live
The way I am, my heart to give
Like the scattered petals buried in the ground
With a broken vine I have found

A broken judgement you have mistaken
A trust you have forsaken
For you walk amid the burning flame
The intention left, what more to gain

I respond, I follow is what you say
To accept and accomplish are left in delay
Shove and push is what you do
When people try to get close to you

So unfair and so discreet
Your mind is set, you're all you need
Not understanding that things may turn
A friendship, a trust, is what you'll learn

If you take the chance you will see
How much you will succeed
Your time and effort are all I ask
Bury the sorrows, for it is the past

This is what life is all about
To question and sacrifice, with some doubt
Set aside the broken past, put it to rest
Consider this as a last request.

By: Giulia Ricciardi
March 16 1994

You

The silence is left for us to stay
For you've gone about to go your way
An ambitious life you've led
A smooth operator, you're in the lead

Your poise is smooth, your words are strong
Your actions have meaning, don't cross him wrong
For hustling he thinks is his trade
This is how his finances are made

But don't get me wrong, this I accept
For your charm is sweet, with a given respect
You have cared for my every need
For what more must I ask of thee

Excitement is what you live for
Your style is what I adore
For me, you are one of a kind
This you should keep in mind

My thoughts maybe lost and confused
All I want to say to you
No matter how hard times may get
My memory of you I shall never forget.

By: Giulia Ricciardi
March 8, 1994

User

Sometimes I wish my heart would skip
The love you gave now a memory bliss
To cherish your heart, I wish to hold
A part you gave me left so cold

How can one give and not feel?
We are human, some left in tears
To use, to run and never look back
Just so cold, this is a fact

As birds may chirp, they may cry
As I lay here to ponder in all your lies
They feed, they're bold, never to forget
Set their paths, fly away at best

I close my eyes, the visions are strong
Convince myself I must move on
The clock will tick loud and clear
Take that second glance, you've disappeared

Someday you'll turn and feel regret
A part of you that you did forget
The thoughts you feel may never part
And reminisce of that broken heart.

By: Giulia Ricciardi
March 18 1994

Curse

As we follow the path of knowledge
We follow it wise to what has been pledged
For we keep in mind of our hurtful thoughts
Never forget the dreadful plot

For who we are is what's been born
To doubt our thoughts is what's been torn
To seek in wonder is our lust
In return you're left in dust

Inside we mourn, that's our sadness
To walk ahead is the test
To hope and pray is what we gain
In return we are left with pain

I weep, I hide, I live in fear
My sadness is left with no one to hear
A child which weeps, a hand in need
With the wind to capture its melody

So, listen wise and hear my piece
To all of you I shall unleash
A forbidden heart inside which bleeds
This curse inside my life will lead

For you to know you must understand
To have the touch of a sacred hand
Which shall unleash the curse upon my heart
And relieve the spell, let the evil part.

By: Giulia Ricciardi
May 31 1994

Obscured

Complexed faces in a complexed time
To journey through searching to be kind
For the touch has froze the unspoken
Imprinted a scar, left a token

Embrace the wind, comfort the soul
Shaken vibes break the cold
The past haunts, leaving its guard intact
While the mind deciphers fiction or fact

Though the body yearns for primitive ground
Sensations flourish over the temptations around
How to calm this need for affection
How to decide on the given intentions

Dangerous stakes with an irresistible power
The yearning bursting inside left to recover
A chance to take but the guard kept high
The uninhibited scent of musk calms the tides.

By: Giulia Ricciardi
July 27 1996

Snapshots of You

Snapshot of this portrait I paint
This image is my undiscovered saint
Unconscious in mind, his reality my fate
Undermined and adored in heaven's place

Free-spirited for his image is strong
His faith feeds his mortal bond
Fallen in place with given haste
Sweet as honey, charmed by his taste

A statute lord in his world awaits
His peace sensed upon, it vindicates
Tears of sorrow meant not to bear
A rebel drifter, bold with flair

Deserted, he shows no pain
The strongest survive the vision in vain
Negative impulses reflect and separate
For his aura left in presence fascinates

Nothing discourages this dreamer released
A mind awakened, in his world to please
Image is solid by strength and mind
Scars inflicted shall fade by time

Snapshots given to this perception envisioned
To foresee this portrait I paint, I have listed
Enlightened by his harmony for its given intention
The message stated, a statured expression.

By: Giulia Ricciardi
July 1999

Deep Inside

Caught my eye in your sight
Dazed and confused in the night
Lonely inside my heart
Wishing for you, not part

Don't be a fool, for I shall repeat
Deep inside do you care for me
In a way, I hope you do
This could be something true

Sometimes I feel so hypnotized
My feelings were kept in disguise
But now you're here, alone with me
A chance to express how I feel

Lonely is what my heart felt
As you, I haven't been able to forget
To uncover the love, I hide
You are the one I wish to be mine

Show your love, show you care
My love I wish for you to bear
Alone, together we are one
In time my heart will come undone.

By: Giulia Ricciardi
February 26, 1994

A Burning Ambition

Though the ring of gold holds the bond
And pictures scatter, the focus is strong
An image passes through the faces that haunt
Though the rainbow's end tease and taunt

The music carries beyond the few
The thoughts are distant between the two
Tempers rise and emotions flaring
A passion unleashed the secret bearing

Longing for that risen ambition
Lusting for the affection given
One night, one touch, my affection
Forgetting all bonds for the vast intentions

An unforsaken touch, the unforbidden love
Craving the hold beyond and above
A touch, a kiss, a time for need
Why torture the heart, why leave it be?

Question the thought, sure, unless knowing
Feeling without scars the soul regretting
For the melody blinds each thought
The sounds carried burns as it begins to launch.

By: Giulia Ricciardi
July 27, 1996

For Love

For who's to say people are all the same
When they all live with sorrow, in pain
To reach out and grab for what they care
To love is a task to bear

Who's to trust for they are all in need
To touch, to hold, my heart may bleed
To love to cherish what does it mean
When all must hurt why must I feel

I am in debt, my life to spare
Especially towards the ones I care
I can hurt, I feel the desperate need
Why must they joke, laugh and tease

For I paid the price I hold despair
As the saying goes life's not fair
I am strong, I will hold on
My life together for I've done some wrong

There's one whom stands and awaits my soul
Whose words are sweet with a heart of gold
I can relate the words are pure
Can I trust again, can I be so sure?

Who's to know such chances we take
I know for sure, no more mistakes
My pain will end, my fun return
As for the past, well, it can burn.

By: Giulia Ricciardi
November 25, 1994

Thief of Hearts

Within a blink of an eye, your life will change
You came to me alone and in pain
I took you in, opened the doors
Not knowing what I was headed for

You conned your way through lies and deceit
Your words were kind, with love so sweet
I gave you all my heart, you took my soul
I gave you my life, you wanted more

You promised me love, you promised me bells
So, I set you free from a life of hell
In return you left a shattered heart
Now it bleeds for you've ripped it apart

I will suffer for my foolish mistakes
For love is blind, I set my own fate
Cold will be the nights you shall foresee
Worthless your love will become left for me.

By: Giulia Ricciardi
December 16, 1993

Mystic Me

Turning around to what we once were
 Wild at heart but not so sure
Escaped from all, had no cares
Once my heart you shared

The looking glass appeared to be
An image of what once was real
Whispers may come, and whispers may go
But who are they to really know?

I once felt, and I paid the price
My life now spins like the dice
To pick and choose who I want
To tease and hurt with pain I taunt

To play them like a child's game
Until it ends, I hold no shame
For they play along just as well
I hold the lead and who's to tell

Shall I ever learn? Will I see the light?
To attack the flesh within the night
I do hunger for their touch
Especially pleasure which I've missed so much

One day I will change, I will learn
The time will come the tables will turn
Nothing's wrong for two hearts accomplish
For what lies ahead beyond that deadly kiss.

By: Giulia Ricciardi
November 11, 1994

Lost Love

As I lay here thinking of you
I reminisce of our last touch
Realizing how I've missed you so much
Left knowing what to do
I never realized until you were gone
My undying love for you has grown

I can feel your soft kisses pass me by
I can feel your strong embrace hold me tight
An emptiness left at stake
The regret to curse and left with hate

For it hasn't been easy lately
There is a missing part of me
Wishing to have expressed myself more
But the fear just took over my soul

In the distance, the nature's cry is what I hear
It reminds of what was once to be
The forbidden pain is what I carried
A hidden secret that I've kept buried

I script this for you, so I can be set free
This secret burdened that has left me in tears
I leave this in your hands
In hoping one day you'll understand

For I believe we shall meet again
In hopes that my heart will mend
Revealing this once more to you
At last you shall know the hidden truth.

By: Giulia Ricciardi
July 30[th,] 1993

Deceived

Liquid ties and twisted hearts
Broken thoughts and shattered parts
Eliminated feelings disguised by expressions
Faded its masked deception

Deceived by the soul, powered by mind
Rainy days shall mask their cries
Though the sorrow shall repair
The image printed shall disappear

The candle burns its flame of life
The sounds of the hidden night
In the eyes left mesmerized
Like blades of steel shining bright

Beneath the stone, beneath the dirt
Shadows pass above the hurt
Whispered lies with hidden lust
Watching over with broken trust

For a moment pass, the passion broken
To scare the heart left a token
To secure its place kept in debt
Left deceived, yet never to forget.

By: Giulia Ricciardi
June 11, 1995

For Hurt

Sometimes I forget what I hold
A person like you so blunt, so cold
How someone like you understand?
Who can help make your heart mend?

I'll forget the pain, I'll forget the sorrow
I'm here today, gone tomorrow
They don't care, they don't see
Who I am, how I feel?

For someday I will be gone
The ones that care, my prayers are strong
I have compassion, I can love
Each time I try my heart breaks in tonnes

Time is precious, I cannot waste
My rage one day they shall taste
In return I'll bring the pain
To the ones who think it's all a game

I will lead, and I will strike
A driven sword with all my might
They will regret, they will see
What the devil inside can really be

Someday will come I will regret
The pain in all for me to forget
I must stay strong, I will return
For myself, lessoned learned.

By: Giulia Ricciardi
November 25, 1994

A Frail Heart

Like visions that burn for a pale heart
A yearning inside that won't part
Though scattered and cold with nowhere to run
To foresee the pain all left undone

Like the rain that falls with no clear destination
This is my path of restoration
For buried in deep, withered and worn
All left to feel is my heart torn

How to escape this path of pain
When all I ask is for some warmth in vain
Though never to pursue or trap the prey
But comfort my soul, as the demon portrayed

To burn in non-existence shall I become
Never to be told, just comfort for one
Though separated, yet I stand
For an image portrayed, heart in hand

Why must it be a giver not a beholder
With emotions astray, I'm left to ponder
For I can feel, yet not able to release
My scattered tears for one to feast

Yet young at heart, maybe weak at points
With a heart that burns to its boiling point
And Image kept strong with followed shame
Yet the fate at hand left the provider's game

By: Giulia Ricciardi
February 27, 1993

Spared Creation

Rain clouds hover and break the shine
For my love for you withers and cries
As every cloud has its place
As my thoughts bleed its taste

I gather each drop and taste its plate
Absorbing each though creates a face
Plaster the mould to its grave domain
I carry its vision carved in vain

Created a bind, released expression
A statute held beyond its haven
No explanation, no picture framed
Only motion thrown, painted engraved

When sunny skies enlighten its frame
It shines so bright, conditioned, it lays
And there released its jacked unknown
But a face beyond a kind never shown

And when it rains, each drop creates
This face unknown the picture paints
There it shines of colours forgiven
My picture painted of a love hidden.

By: Giulia Ricciardi
November 3, 1998

Crossed by the Heart

Broken glass with shallow walls
Hidden pasts of ragged dolls
Unleashed the thought carried on
Why must it scare, why can't I be strong

Shaded crosses and ribbon ties
Painful sculptures, forbidden cries
To terminate this feeling hidden
To accelerate this desire that's given

To fade the words of spoken minds
The absence of the sands of time
To run beyond the fields of joy
A fondled heart played like a toy

The dream carried like a lust that burns
Though reality stands as the world turns
The child within released by day
As the demon inside sneaks and preys

My soul becomes poisoned and weak
My match to make my heart shall seek
For my will is strong, my courage bold
A leader shall rise with the strength of gold.

By: Giulia Ricciardi
September 1995

Scents of Life

Sometimes we hold in our pain
To show it is all but in shame
To hide behind closed doors
The looking glass holds our souls

To escape is the greatest task
To let go of the forbidden past
The darkness will once shine
For in lasting pain, all in time

Sometimes we must all forget
To receive the lonely hand, held in debt
To deepen the sorrow, wish the touch
Your softened words, I miss that much

I shall stand by, I will listen
Your lips that preach of words which glisten
To live your dream to its very best
For your love to show may prove your test

You hear me but far beyond
A memory to hold, your heart will bond
For the looking glass shall once appear
Your soul will once again be destined, free.

By: Giulia Ricciardi
November 14, 1994

True Words

For who's to say that passion fades
When separated from the bed that's made
Once held, once loved
Never to push, never to shove

For who's to say to lust is wrong
Once it's made, the separation is gone
When unleashed the need is carried
Absorbing its moment, the pain buried

Two hearts so pure, yet so far away
For the time spent fills the delay
Yet some words unleashed may be so cold
But we keep inside what's been told

To touch, to want, to love, to lust
To hold, to need your heart I trust
No riches, no gifts your heart I don't buy
My actions, my words, my heart is no lie

For who's to say the truth is forbidden
When it hurts more just kept hidden
My words are true, my love is pure
This I keep in my heart secure.

By: Giulia Ricciardi
February 10, 1995

Reminisce

Can you remember when we were together
Thought we would last forever
The fun and games without the pain
Wish it were still the same

A walk in the park
Love straight from the heart
Thought it would never end
No more broken heart to mend

Now there are no more sunny days
For you're gone, left your own way
You wanted to set new tracks
But I knew someday you'd turn back

Though you're still around
With another love you have found
For it will never be the same
You said it was part of the game

Someday you will return to me
For you wanted to be set free
My love for you has been released
For now, you are a memory buried deep.

By: Giulia Ricciardi
February 26, 1994

Alone

Alone is what my heart feels
Love is what my heart bleeds
To live, to care is my regret
To love you I must forget

Something which I must escape
Only hope can set my fate
If only my soul could shine
If only you were mine

Hopeless is what I feel
Reality, this must be real
I reach, you turn away
My heart you've placed in pain

Alone my heart is buried
Alone the hurt shall carry
If you only knew how much I've lost
To follow this path, I've crossed

To wither away and fall to pieces
My soul shall drift away, understand this
You are as cold as they come
My heart has come undone

For you've blown from dust to wind
You alone have left my heart unhinged
You came crashing in like waves colliding
Alone I feel, I've gone into hiding.

By: Giulia Ricciardi
March 18, 1994

Drifted Off

Drifting like mist in the air
I'm lost in time, ask if I care
Thoughts are in a daze
Life's just like a never-ending maze

Drifting like the clouds
Everything is spinning round and round
Am I lost? When will it end?
Who cares really? My pain will mend

To gather up all that hurts
My life feels like it's been cursed
A chain wrapped around my heel
For my high is what I feel

The flame shall keep burning
My world will keep turning
Just a word to the wise
I'm feeling just fine.

By: Giulia Ricciardi
September 1994

Stoned Thoughts

Tainted pictures in the sky
As I gaze on my backside
Shooting stars over head
God, I feel as if I'm dead
Sweet melodies are what I hear
Soft Whispers chanting: I feel no fear
Beat, beat, my heart starts to go
Drip, Drip the sweats starts to pour
Hypnotized by the night
Mesmerized by the lights
Painted pictures flash in my mind
Felt as if I've travelled back in time
Take a breath of air
Take it deep if you dare
Chirp, Chirp, the birds go
Swish, swish, the world goes
Feel the breeze pass by
I feel at ease, flying high
Not yet ready to say goodbye
So, for you who've missed the fun
Jokes on you, it's all gone.

By: Giulia Ricciardi

Lost in a Dream

Watching in the distance, this traffic of emotions
Feeling like a bird, guided by its devotion
Melodies carried along, each lyric whispered
Finding its harmony subsides what's hindered

Lost in direction, searching for signs of freedom
An unexplored loss feeding redemption
A smoke cloud starts to hover around me
Floating, a release starts to find my energy

An image paints my direction ahead
Negativity has drifted, its pride had to end
Self-indulged, I've become absorbed by all
For the hands touching release the darken fall

So fresh, it's cleansed my soul, restored my charm
Like the sunshine after the rain, my heart is warm
My eyes brightened like treasures of gold
Have I been found from these lyrics told?

The melodies have changed my path of direction
Feeling I have been guided by this resurrection
The visions left tainted in a mass reflection
And the whispers faded, hypnotized by its translation

A dream has its beginnings yet no endings maybe so
Fairy tales have Prince Charming and treasures of gold
The hands of time melted and captured by glass
Maybe this never-ending story has been just a task.

By: Giulia Ricciardi
May 15, 2004

Alive

Sometimes when the dark is numb
I come undone
To the breath of the morning fire
My love is set to your desires

Like an angel above
Soft as the white dove
A spirit carried
To the love I kept buried

Now it's time to come alive
Before your time passes by
Left for your fate
What more must it take

This may be your only chance
To make the lovers dance
Follow its melody
It will take you to its destiny

Like the hidden pain
Its time to try again
Like a song that flows forever
For we are meant to be together.

By: Giulia Ricciardi
October 28, 1993

Embraced

I held a crystal, which visions enlisted
Its peaceful bond of two depicted
Embodied myself to grasp such love
Like the owl soars, like the peaceful dove

Darkened skies have hovered your soul
A loss of despair has taken its toll
Though I stand aside, wicked in vain
I weep in silence, embracing your pain

Bizarre is life, its endings we fear
New beginnings arise, and new souls appear
To define itself becomes new lyrics
Expressed beyond the spirits lifted

Landed souls we've become as one
Finding its peace, a given undone
I follow, I guide, preach the unforgiven
Embracing the hurt, unleashing what's hidden

Only one can capture the unexpected
A soul that drifted, a soul neglected
And its findings shall comfort its peace
Alas, my prayer once again unleashed.

By: Giulia Ricciardi
November 16, 1998

Friendship

Time has passed so quickly
  Our friendship still holds between you and me
Through the laughter, through the tears
I'm grateful you're still here

Whenever I was distressed or feeling blue
I always knew to turn to you
You have helped me the best you can
Been the first to lend a hand

For there was a time you had to leave
And our friendship tore to pieces
The reasons I'll never forget
A time in which I do regret

An empty space stayed deep inside
No one left for me to confide
For we were so close, so alike
How we let it end over a fight

Then one day you returned
The broken past was left to burn
And the bond started once again
A solid friendship was to gain

Now we are rarely ever left apart
Set off to a fresh new start
But there is something you must know
Before the time comes where we must go

You have been a part of my life
Without you I would have died
In hopes our friendship stays together
Through laughter and tears, with love forever.

By: Giulia Ricciardi
February 25, 1994

My Valentines

Valentine's, such a day to remember
   With gifts to loves signed, always and forever
A moment in time which people cherish
Some laughs, some cries, some fulfilled its wishes

With me it comes with no surprise
The time of year which makes me cry
For I haven't had, tried at will
Someone to share my heart to fulfill

Now I will take this chance
To go beyond a step in advance
An understanding I will accept
Our friendship will stand, don't forget

For you are the one that has been charmed
The one I choose, one I want, no harm
You must understand this is the test
To fulfill that special Valentine's Request

You're so in depth, yet so discreet
Embodied is your soul, looks from the deep
To be subjective, please don't manipulate
With no hesitation, just to complicate

Valentine's day, that special day to please
When all attractions and expressions unleashed
A day so special, a day that's known
For all hearts to warm, it's all in the tone.

By: Giulia Ricciardi
February 14, 1995

Elements of You

For all that was lost you have found
For all the sadness carried you bound
You made a home with open arms
You shed your knowledge, left your charm

Your words keep our survival, share emotions
Your beliefs were strong, friendship a devotion
Your spirit carried for all who knew
An influence passed along the few

A solider armed for any given war
Shining colours enhanced from heaven afar
Like a rainbow in the clouds that shift
Its colours last for a given time

Always remembered, always in thought
For your lyrics preached leaves their mark
Shine above is what you do best
All are touched, you've completed your quest

A chip of laughter, a breath of air
Your heart given fresh, your touch of care
Your weakness in emotions felt in drifts
Once repressed have now released

Feel your vibe, all not lost in time
You're a solider with given pride
With open arms your knowledge in the end
Outlasts with charm, a warrior's friend.

By: Giulia Ricciardi
November 11, 2002

Path of Light

As I close my eyes, visions start to undress
Thoughts received left to be expressed
In desperate attempts I try to separate
A past beyond which haunts and regenerates

Soft whispers drift and calm the soul
A touch of grace embraces the cold
The visions enlisted, to some a pawn
The dawn of kings, who protect their spawn

The scars are deep, wounds kept strong
To break these walls, a place to belong
For the nights are dark, pitch is black
Which makes the days a signature mask?

There ahead lies a light for every tunnel
An angel beyond there who casts a funnel
Trying to absorb and bless forgiveness
For the darkened hearts to lay their nest

Destiny is set with broken pathways
Carved in stone is a direction laid
For that red carpet, life's reflection painted
A mirror of shine which blesses the tainted

Allowing oneself to become one with shame
To bury the past, retrieve its game
You will shine to what lies ahead
Your soul will embrace and aid its mend.

By: Giulia Ricciardi
April 2001

A Promised Land

Like an enchanted land with a promised hand
A bell that rings is the sound of a newborn thing
Heal the wound of a lonely heart
Only love will never tear them apart

With the holy shine of the morning light
Soft voices flare, through the day and night
The flowers bloom over the land of promise
The trees stand tall, bold and modest

A beautiful sound from the birds that sing
They fly high with the stroke of their wings
As the daybreak falls and the sun sets down
The song from birds stops, left with the cricket's sound

The night is here, and the stars are out
As they glimmer and shine and dance about
The two set out prepare the night's fire
Fulfill the dark with their deepest desires

Their heart beating fast, loud and strong
For this is where they belong
Their love is full and set free
As they take their night to ecstasy

As the crack of dawn is about to appear
The sounds of the birds are loud and clear
The sweet sounds of a soft melody
For they are on to fulfill their destiny

Like the enchanted land with a promised hand
Awaiting to hear the bell that rings
For that is the sound of a newborn thing
Healed the wound of a lonely heart
Their love shall never tear them apart.

By: Giulia Ricciardi
October 17, 1993

Scattered Heart

Though a decision kept by heart
   Kings and queens torn apart
Intoxicated by the mind
Not to leave the past behind

Infection by the play at hand
Driven to a sacred land
The one and only a difference in play
A shallow life through the past may prey

To believe and hope beyond the time
To leave behind the peace inside
Not to change the night given
But to accept the pain hidden

And never to show the unleashed
To give and take from the pleased
Just to hold on, that chance
To forsake that second glance

Fondled by these words portrayed
To persist a truth never played
A forgotten bliss amongst the dark
The child's game played in the park

To learn and live on as believed
Amongst the ones who deceived
Though alone and on my own
By words, who cares, my heart still carries on.

By: Giulia Ricciardi
April 5, 1996

Dissolved

A razor's edge is our lifeline
For it cuts so deep and so fine
And unexpected, it trails away
While we watch as it sets its delay

As we absorb such pain, forgetting our existence
We embellish the thought of resistance
For the ores which are symbolic to one's being
May be exotic to one's teasing

A mystic gaze will empower our vision
Which reflects on each decision
Though expressions made by impulse
Diminish the truth, avow it's false

Adapted myself is what I've become
Redeeming oneself, rejection for some
A primitive ground set by purpose
Inflicted by one's desired thirst

Our bodies mesmerized by inflicted ties
The visions left of coloured skies
A satisfied desire beyond compare
Our souls have drifted, the pain is spared.

By: Giulia Ricciardi
July 25, 1997

Captured Soul from a Heart of Darkness

A captured soul with demon eyes
A heart of darkness sheds no cries
An evil touch is what he holds
A kiss so deadly, with words so cold

For death hangs over him, this beware
A chance to take, your heart he'll tear
He feeds on pain, blood's his thirst
A power withheld, with a deadly curse

His prey is weak, young at heart
Awaits in time for the sky to part
The moon is full, big and bright
As the reflections of his demon eyes

His shadow haunts when you're asleep
Whispers words to trance the weak
If your soul is captured, there's no return
As your weakened soul is left to burn.

By: Giulia Ricciardi
September 1994

The Dominant vs The Unknown

White lies and broken promises
Darkened nights and twisted myths
Passionate kisses and shattered trust
Self image exposed, forbidden lust

An animal grows inside my soul
Lurking the grounds, lusting more
Shattered from dreams to its reality
Not knowing, killing my integrity

Ambitious and innocent like a child
Self-portrayed free and wild
Words which trance the dangerous minds
Touch is soft captured by the eyes

A soul which travels the lands
A soul that understands
Is it the image portrayed?
So naïve by the game played

Am I lying to myself, so blinded?
A lonely soul fooled by a fabricated mind
Struck by lighting and broken by thunder
In the end, the dominant stays stronger.

By: Giulia Ricciardi
Sept 5, 1995

Chaos of Love

To throw all patterns of you out my way
To take my heart, to be with you today
Despite your eyes, white lies and shade
A picture not so perfect, shimmers and fades

Amused, the mind tries to flee, maybe absorbed
Disillusioned, yet reality becomes confirmed
I find my reasons to maybe appease
Yet once done our minds set at ease

A niche, maybe tasked hiding, searching
Pain endured becomes useful, it's binding
Change becomes an essence, yet I think of you
Poisoned by darkened thoughts, I'm consumed

I reflect different shadows, some unaware
Controlled, I find my world lost, yet I'm scared
Lost, I endure such expectations not needed
Bounded, I felt betrayed, feeding desperation

You've inflicted emotions I can't compromise
I find a fear which feeds and hypnotizes
I'm off balance, lured an unexpected direction
All I want is harmony and to feel protected

Guide my soul, let breath feel my essence
Protect my mind, don't let it separate, let it dance
Passion with love and trust I've yet to learn
Maybe I will find my love, what I yearn.

By: Giulia Ricciardi
June 2004

Lost Fantasy

To all I have seen, to all that I have heard
An image, a message sent to be absorbed by words
I unfold words sent, I translate, I make no sense
In all theory there has become an absence

Follow, you may portray an image profound
I've found myself, my belongings no longer bound
Moment came, and you fled like the pull given by time
You have yet to understand this spirit so divine

I task, I linger, I feed off your given intentions
Yet in return I feel no given direction
The sun has set, such a given pace it heeds
A passion disguised by the masks in deed

Feel the rebellion living inside, it screams
Controlled, it finds a balance, it redeems
Stolen, I ripped beyond a spirit existed
Though acceptance seems to be restricted

So, I follow this journey towards my life's extreme
A world so absorbed, a world drowning in dreams
It follows a pattern, it memorizes each thought
For it carries you, its visions create a plot

A vision of beauty, a symphony of fire, my goddess
Cursed to my own reflection, my freedom, my emptiness
Pandora's box released a melody, to its poison in reality
My fight, my pride, my given integrity lost in fantasy.

By: Giulia Ricciardi
June 2004

Torch on Fire

Quench that thirst which poisons my veins
The yearning thrusts my blood, deepens the pain
Like the nails clamped to each part
Driven mad by this lust of art

The liquid red tainted my pores
Like a loose demon of a wicked whore
Surrounded by darkness, hunger of flesh
Grasping with force to unleash this mess

My lips are soft like sweetened rose
My touch scattered with its creative poise
The bite released absorbs each part
With its thirst: left a bleeding heart

An arousal hit to its boiling point
Erupting each body part; cracking joints
Last, its stimulating pace becomes erotic
Unwind with no words, its motion platonic

A melody of pounding hearts; cries of satisfaction
A hunger for the taste of that simple affection
For soft as silk, and sheer as satin
Unguarded, the flow separates the attraction

Take me to this ecstasy with no end
Absorb each function; its hunger needs a mend
Cure this thirst, magnetized through the veins
For the arousal given receives the erotic drain.

By: Giulia Ricciardi
August 19, 1997

Awaiting the Mystic

I'm left to die in your hands
To end the pain, to make amends
Take its soul, follow its path
In mystic ways love shall last

Death-defying, the thought of you leaving
For my heart shall cry, deepen its bleeding
If you only knew to follow my lead
You would understand the passion I need

To choose, to find, what is the case?
A challenge in all we must face
To force, to push is not my way
Not the kind to tease and play

My heart is pure, my words are deep
Without you by my side my soul won't sleep
Never to trust is the promise that's kept
For your sorrow holds a painful debt

I will send for you and await your answer
With no hesitation until your heart is sure
So, I will listen for you until it's time
For that day will come and you are mine.

By: Giulia Ricciardi
November 20, 1994

Scattered Image

For every lyric spoken turns to a melody
Every note pitched receives a harmony
An escape bound to its perception
The embrace ponders to its reception

Enhance a vision unspoken to its release
Its emotion given bleeds to its embrace
Mesmerized by the portrait's reflection
Bonded towards its given infection

I linger beyond any domain
I feel your need, I bleed your pain
Unmistaken and given such boldness
To grasp such emotion seeks kindness

Unleash a faith, its peace I give
For in belief I am a life which lives
My soul shall scatter a piece I lay
A question to how long, I must dismay

A melody I follow, its harmony I swallow
Sweet as its charm I am now hollow
How to escape its sorrow enhanced
I read in mind, I turn to glance

I drink this wine, bleed its taste
The direction followed sets its face
Its pattern given portrays such haste
Behind any domain I reach this peaceful place.

By: Giulia Ricciardi
June 1999

It's About....

The smell of your sweet lips still lingers
Time has passed so fast, yet I still hinder
Sometimes I feel as if I'm just a page away
Things might just fall, is it my place to stay?
I hear your voice and it makes me shiver
Just to hear you speak makes me quiver
It's all about my play

I see my place and it sets a fear in me
Just knowing it can't be real, I leave
And I know I can't keep thinking that way
But it hurts to just believe its my day
And I know the time will come as we grow
Why forget it, maybe its my destiny, so I follow
It's about being real

Been down many roads, its been a rough ride
I've changed my direction, find the bright side
I love a good fairy tale, need to stay in reality
Who doesn't love a good story, I drift into fantasy
Can't help it feel like a kid, maybe I'm not ready
It's about making mistakes, right? Keep it steady
It's about belief

I'll give myself to you, I don't have to justify
I'll give this a shot, for this I just can't deny
You come along my way and I tingle inside
You make my heart beat, so I go for the ride
And who am I kidding, it's you that I'm wanting
Inside I just can't seem to stop laughing
It's about to get real.

By: Giulia Ricciardi
May 2007

Aiding the Mend

Sometimes a pain inside wants to explode
A distance in thought beyond my control
Emotions in a mix where the bond is broken
The lighting struck mistaken as the given token

The flame that's risen meant for all reasons
Lifted from the grounds of all seasons
Smokes laid, and ashes may fall
Forgiveness, the word known by all

If the chance carried is left beyond recognition
Then confusion is left with the given decisions
To see beyond how no one cares
Amongst the ones left here to bear

For words are spoken but nothing's heard
How to express what's inside to what's learned
The tremors inside hold on to your deception
A jigsaw puzzle left to your perception

A piece in heart, a peace in mind
A blocked road just to proceed the blind
Hoping for that chance to crash through again
Breaking the stone, aiding the mend.

By: Giulia Ricciardi
April 24, 1996

Scattered Thoughts

A light upon my shoulder
Held with embrace is its boulder
Endure the compassion given
Though barricaded is a passion hidden

Its delicate movement enhances its sight
Its depth and devotion strengthen by light
A source we call upon to protect
What more to believe, less we forget

A rise may behold, the image cold
Intended its course strong and bold
Caged is the perceptive we give
For it withdraws from which it's intended

So, we grasp its bond, take what's weak
A profound conclusion tended to unleash
You break its mould, touch its soul
Drive it deep through its shaken tole

Left to satisfy its driven pain
An immature passion is its gain
A smell so sweet it weakens the curse
A fight beyond the sound, it's rest assured

A wicked spirit has become, yet it stands
A wish given keeps its pride at hand
Each grasp it takes withholds a need
Somehow, above all, the picture endures the dream.

By: Giulia Ricciardi
September 19, 1997

My Prayer

As she lays her head to rest, the spirits hover
Though darkness surrounds her, emotions uncover
No words are spoken for the tears flooded
For what's inside has become uncovered

Like the strands of time that fall never-ending
Like the cuts that bleed, waiting to be mended
Though the shadows remain and haunt her cold
She prays to the Gods above to spare her soul

A trail of other's pain, longing for the exception
Deserted heart felt, given the wrong intentions
The visions are clear there's nowhere to reach
Nowhere to hide her pain left for keeps

The prayer in thought to enchant her peace
To secure her well-being from her life of deceit
To burst into laughter, to chant into melody
To feel as one, to claim her own destiny

What solution will conquer the darkness she bears
What grace will mend this heart of despair
Who will spark the candle and give her light?
Who will awaken the soul from the shadows lurking the night?

Diminish the thoughts and tend the pain
Unleash her heart, vanish the shame
Speak the words, wipe the tears
Your destined dream will conquer its fears.

By: Giulia Ricciardi
June 22, 1996

Black Raven

Black raven poisoned my blood
Black lies turned to mud
Given demands which proceed to lies
Broken hands which burn the eyes

Purity and pride flushed to the sea
To play the fool driven by its plea
To part the hate within
To accept the life caused by sin

Scraping through the walls surrounding
Swimming through the dirt that's drowning
Ripping the thread that holds the wound
Which mends the flesh of its cursed burn?

Like the hurt that stains the heart
Blessed upon the purest part
Peace I can never have, left in doubt
An entrance with no way out

What ruins the path which holds the feast?
The black raven's curse has unleashed
What drives the soul to be cold-hearted?
As it glides above, finish what it's started

Black raven has taken over
Flesh and bone, carved in stone, pure
Black raven a feast for desire
Its strength poisoned to admire.

By: Giulia Ricciardi
February 21, 1996

Poisoned

Embody yourself with the visions in your mind
Hypnotized by the colors of fire, left behind
You're burnt out, your body feels weak
For death to all is the question we seek

The poison runs throughout your veins
Making it difficult for the mind to stay sane
Yet so enlightened by the images
Of such tainted walls your emotions hidden

Your body sweats feel the rush burning
Focus on the good, your mind is turning
Filled with broken thought, mixed emotions
Your soul is drifting to another dimension

A twisted truth to what we feel
For all we know this could be real
A feeling carried through our time
Somehow, we have released the poison inside.

By: Giulia Ricciardi
March 1995

One in Darkness

In darkness they have become one
For they have no fear, their time is done
Words are few, for what's preached is death
They preach with meaning, there's nothing left

The dark is their light, the music their soul
Their minds are knowledge, their poise is cold
As death becomes them, I sit in fear
Portraying an image of sorrow with no tears

One's motions carried by thoughts released
Understand in depth, their words, their beliefs
With rattling chains and beats of tremor
Another world in mind, to destruct in terror

What will become of one in darkness?
With the minds of death, life is pointless
For they walk amid the burning flame
To portray their kind, life's just a game.

By: Giulia Ricciardi
July 24, 1994

Land of the Dead

They say the land of the living is the land of the dead
For souls are cursed and souls are walking with no end
Sounds are heard, whispers are chanting
The dead have not rested in peace, the living ranting

Buildings that are torched are nothing but ashes
As it burns in flames the evil hatches
The dead awaken, and the souls are singing
For the broken ties of a new beginning

We walk the ridged path beneath the broken skies
Its destination unknown, as for its death's cry
Our guide will follow, and we shall learn
Beyond the path where the buildings burn

To gaze upon the land in red
Where the living cry in the land of the dead
The sky poisoned by its thickened stream
The cries grow louder by shattered dreams

Where shall we go, what will become of us
Until nothing is left, and we burn to dust
Will we shed no tears, our courage stays strong?
Our guide will carry our soul where we belong.

By: Giulia Ricciardi
November 10, 1994

Awakening Soul

The leaves sway with the flow of the wind
The sun shines as the morning birds sing
Waiting to see what tomorrow brings
This is the time where change is everything

The sky darkens as the sea starts to part
You've opened the soul of a lonely heart
It was kept hidden for so long
You've started its beat, now it beats strong

You've uncovered the worst, I feel no pain
You've set me free by breaking these chains
You've set the love in me alive
Now there's nothing left to hide

The leaves sway with the flow of the wind
The sun shines as the morning birds sing
The sky is bright blue and clear
No more sadness, no more tears.

By: Giulia Ricciardi
August 1st, 1993

Justice Laid

A proposal is what I lay
One can take it for all its dismay
A spirit found left forgiven
For its portrait a confession hidden

As it's said, her words are her whispers
To understand is a written prescription
Lyrics spun in a lost world
Who's to say she portrays a blur

To understand her given domain
To foresee the heart that's been slain
A darkness lifted, a peace she prays
Treat and heal her spirit healed

Purify this darkened soul
For a mortal, like clay can mould
So delicate a sculpture in the past
Release her secrets, let her last

Take her trust find the pain
Lay it down to separate, make her tame
Control her thoughts, relax her image
A prize felt priceless, though primitive

Design her body, feed the spirit
This mortal angel confronted, lifted
Guide her heart, brighten the mind
In return a solid love you shall find.

By: Giulia Ricciardi
July 2001

Complete

Imagine a thought, how could it be
When I close my eyes, so complete
I find its soul set as its peace
Yet only its visions keep it at ease

No touch no kiss could compare
For it's not physically felt to bear
Your sorrow your heart expressed
Through each door bearing is compressed

Repressed a heart broken and shattered
Replenished its fate, unconditionally scattered
For only one could find its part
Every soul separated from the start

Crossings will always overcome its barrier
For life holds a threatened terror
We journey its path, know to follow
Not realizing our characters are hollow

Filled to believe once loved, once touched
Yet to foresee lust is the painted blush
Each life has its own destiny buried
To find its light extends the identity carried

Embraced myself with each lyric spoken
Empowered by thoughts, your love left broken
Scared my flesh replenish by an illusion
Complete, so divine you've given self redemption.

By: Giulia Ricciardi
July 8 1998

Signs of Affection

I know a place deep inside my heart
An unpaved road leading nowhere finds a part
Hidden signs ahead caution if you dare
Enlighten your eyes, its image unfair

This sensation that is felt becomes wrong
For I am running and your presence felt strong
Trying to find you to get you alone
This feeling that's kept inside has become known

We can hang by the waters, chat 'til dawn
Let our emotions run wild, feed their spawn
The music shall set a peaceful melody
Unleashing our souls, dancing in harmony

A magic carpet ride above the skies
As we ponder, over hearts left hypnotized
Dance with me forever, a moment so divine
The consequences encountered a treasured find

The sense to scream, I need to heal
I can feel its essence, lost in its ecstasy
Unleash the fear, forget its sin, light its fire
As we become one our souls drift in desire

By: Giulia Ricciardi
March 8 2004

Stay

Turning around back then
   To the times we became close friends
You spoke wild, you were drifted
Where your mind was lifted

Considered life as an open gamble
For girls then were in shambles
And when you aid, you don't care
She stood by your side, unaware

Disguised your image by a few
Didn't love, didn't even care to
She stood by like a child
Lost in dreams of colour so wild

You became one for awhile
For lust was your only desire
And when she said she cared
You pushed her away, not to dare

You asked her to stay 'til the night's fall
Stay until the morning's call
Just stay and fill my lust
Stay 'til my heart can trust

They were apart yet so close
Their hearts led a sacred toast
They became one once again
For wild hearts with no shame

Child's play and tainted minds
Left them racing to the hands of time
And if you paid attention you would see
Two shaded souls famed to believe

For words and time spent by all
The introduction of future falls
For broken ties mended strong
A blessing of a sacred bond.

By: Giulia Ricciardi
April 4 1995

Note to Self

Every day becomes such a battle
Constant arguments of life's scenarios
To get frustrated, of course, it's a hassle
To feel disregarded, that's my story

Save yourself the embarrassment
We all have stories, issues of the past
It's just relentless, I know you're spent
You're the one that makes it last

Take a second look, take a breath
When you're alone, reflect on your greatness
The past is what you left
You're the one making it relentless

Kind of sick of all the negativity
Kind of sick of all the mental bullying
I've done my time with all your abuse
Come to realize it's people like you
Save your words, save your thoughts
It'll just come back one day to haunt
So, please, with all due respect
Take a second look before you regret
We all have secrets in which we keep
Do you really wish for me to repeat?

So, it may not be my personality
I must say I'm feeling a bit expressive
Do you feel that maybe it's reality?
Maybe this is coming across excessive

Must have been mistaken, a little clouded
A judgement call left unspoken
To ever think you were empowered
Maybe forgotten, always the reflection

Give your head a shake, must be poison
Look at yourself before you forget
This is what you envisioned
This is your true reality, your destiny
You've come to play, you've already set.

By: Giulia Ricciardi
March 20, 2014

A Picture

They say a picture says a thousand words as it shows
But then again assumption seems to the ones that know
It all depends what it's trying to portray as depicted
Heck, we can all take a guess, but it's the emotion enlisted
A picture stands still for what does it really show?
Pick any conclusion, make a story up, come on, let's go

It's not intimidating once you play along, catch the flow
There's much to guess out there, turn it into a show
Just play along and let's create some new memories
At the end of the day, not hurting anyone, young and free
For who's to say to act your age, who are they, boring at best
For complicated as it seems here let's put it to the test

I see this face, marked by the journey, a long road ahead
He seems willed to take on any challenge to what's led
He's strong and empowered, though emotionally barred
This man I see in this picture, has some deep scars
For nevertheless, there is beauty in all that we seek
Look deep into their eyes, understand the story they reap

No journey is graceful by any means, this I know
I've experienced myself, the emotional scars to show
But I pushed on through the warrior in me must rise
Life's full of choices, it's the sacrifices that compromise
We protect the ones who are most important to us
We stand our ground to the ones who betray our trust

A picture says a lot of words for us to strongly repeat
It seems to have a different story to tell, from what I see
A special moment in time that may hold to us dear
Or a drastic change in life to that journey, that leap
So, take my hand, shut up, just share the applause
Picture this moment in time, relax yourself just because.

By: Giulia Ricciardi

The Visions I See

I have a million reasons not to say what I really want
What I feel inside is just a mimic of emotions that haunt
I close my eyes and these lucid visions come to sight
I toss and turn, losing sleep from shadows that bite
The story tells a thousand words, nothing seems right
Blasted all to hell I'm wishing to just sleep at night

It's become a slight obsession, the reason to decipher
These images I seem to portray, I need a solider for hire
For lord only knows what will happen if I threw stones
Maybe he can find its balance, maybe he can set the tone
For now, it's as I predicted, a message which comes to me
Careful, the steps I take, the bridges I burn, people I seek

A moment to own is my talent in which I can rise above
A dangerous road that leads, there are no mourning doves
No magical wand to sway and no crystal balls at play
A place of illusions and journeys is the message portrayed
So, strap on my boots and away I go and try to figure out
When I lay my head down, play out this fear and its doubts

The people here are all so different with lots in motion
This place changes quickly, so vast with lots of commotion
One minute I'm in a house climbing up a variety of stairs
Next, I'm outside running through forests trees so bare
Sometimes I'm being chased down, in a fight or torn apart
At times someone's in distress asking for help, play my part

The visions never last long, but takes it toll when I sleep
I wake up thinking "dear god where the hell have, I been"
Though it takes me a moment to come back to reality
My body could be trembling at times, sweating profusely
Then the deciphering begins, and a reason to start my task
Where's my pen and paper, create another story at last.

By: Giulia Ricciardi

Linger

A whisper chanting in my thoughts
Distracting each move, it's possessive and taunts
To separate is the fight, breaking all ties
Though paralyzes with soft touches and warm cries

River of cold running through my veins
Pounding drums rhythm my heart with strain
As my eyes weep mortal tears
I stand alone with darkened fears

For I realize a missing link is what I yearn
Until understood, profound and it burns
My heart is opened to all directions
Once touched it fears the infection

So I linger in this loss of despair
I restrain and try to regain beyond compare
But these whispers control and emotions collide
Seduced by its quiet spell is it defies

This dying moon with a river of cold
A fury of longing to become so bold
As I strive to exist, it captures my thoughts
Forcing direction of a link, it taunts

Entrap myself in this room without a view
I gather my thoughts, which left are few
And I wish to the skies without stars
Help find this missing link from afar.

By: Giulia Ricciardi
September 20, 1997

Confucius

Hidden from a place never been
Hidden the fact never seen
Though the thread stills mends
The truth still out there, it pretends

Though the wound inside weeps
The doubt holds it keep
To hold on strong, I've prayed
Though intentions have been laid

For that kiss that fell in hand
Wishing to be swept to a destined land
My heart holds a place of hurt
Never to return to where it lurks

Possibly regretting all that has past
Hoping and wishing it never lasts
For a barrier still stands in line
Frightened to cross, dominated by ties

Personal, yet modest by its confusion
Only to be left by an illusion
An unbelief in a barricaded time
Crept in front of the future's pride

To express, to comfort, to be loved once
Why must it question, why I must doubt
Though patience is a virtue, I long to give
Peace to my heart so a passion can live.

By: Giulia Ricciardi
Sept 10, 1996

Passive Bearing

I carry myself towards my domain
My thought resurfaces the burden of shame
Such a constant force of action
Which, thrives for a stable satisfaction

I desire the strength to overcome such infliction
As for a solution never comes in my direction
To pardon myself to live at ease
But it falls and scatters, never to please

To become like the wind and drift away
Like the leaves which move to its dismay
Like the clouds which hover over the moon
Somehow its shine replenishes its tomb

Carry me like the wind that drifts
Let my heart shine no matter where it sets
For I can no longer settle and linger in doubt
My temperature is rising; it yearns for a way out

Days go by, seasons change, time just drifts
Infinite with regression, Casanova is a myth
So genuine so passive, a picture painted deep
And someday shall resurface its defeat.

By: Giulia Ricciardi
October 1997

A Hope and Prayer

Windows always appear, the reflections we fear
They set an image we can't replace
Beyond the cause of our broken tears
An existence we have held in place

Tangled to believe in a love beyond
Though never pondered to its depth
An energy broken so strong
A power we have kept in strength

To fight, we become weak and break
Kept back a fantasized thought
For we fall, our heart aches
Yet all we feel is the game we bought

Like the prey, we embellish, never again
The path set explains our soul
It set the anger and grows with pain
Engraved is the sorrow we bear to unfold

A sense made to this explained
Yet questions are answers to its demand
For I explained, but hold in the pain
Left all in pieces, hoping you'll understand.

By Giulia Ricciardi
April 30, 1997

I'm Still Waiting

When the stars come out at night, the spirits cry
Voices screaming, their time has set aside
The sun may rise with a new beginning
A pattern starts to set, a new fate has risen

Your words feed my thoughts, your heart is bold
Your presence surrounds me, I feel so cold
For the past has left its scar my world has risen
To all who come before you left forbidden

Resistant you stand, nothing can break you
You're far gone now, hate has become you
For an honest soul may cross your path
But you'll turn away, unleash your wrath

No way, no how can this ever become
What reasons given you chose to run
Its useless to just believe there was a chance
Someone was willing to give, just a second chance

So, when the stars come out, my tears may fall
In my deepest sleep, I feel the burden, sense it all
I'm fighting a battle to justify the ending
Believe in me, I say, I will be waiting.

By: Giulia Ricciardi

It's Your Life

How do you mend a heart in pain?
Which cries in fear, pours like rain
How do you stop the fights, the crime?
When will they learn the prize is time?

Trying to understand them, I listen, I learn
Each time I hear, their bodies left to burn
I write these words, try to preach the knowledge
As we see no one cares to what's been pledged

The movies the music, it's all the same
For all they see, their life's a game
No one cares what they must show
The pride is gone, turned to drugs they know

The streets are their homes, their only palace
No sunshine left, no more smiles on faces
They have built their kingdom in their minds
This is the life of choice to grind

They cannot see what lies ahead
The ones they hurt, the pain they shed
I guess this is their story to tell
Hard to watch their lives turn to hell.

By: Giulia Ricciardi
June 30, 1994

Gang War

He starts so innocent, young at heart
He takes day by day, one step at a time
He watches the city streets with one thing in mind
Death is all he knows, war is all he sees
Blood on blood is his trade, pain is what he's made
What or how to stop his rage you ask
A question to all, a question of task

The gang war begins in the hot summer nights
Beneath the city lights
Bang, down he goes
Drip, drip as the blood flows
A soft tear falls down his face
As none are left in sight, gone without a trace
Left to bleed in the hot summer nights

Our children are dying each day
From the games that these gangs play
Shoot to kill is what they do
Graves to dig with sorrow for me and you
Now who's the fool I say
Who's the strong one now
Have you accomplished your vow?

Take it from me, a gang war is not the place to be
For I am young at heart
Would disintegrate if you were to part
For we leave behind the cup of tears
As we drift apart down the red sea.

By: Giulia Ricciardi
July 29, 1993

Higher Learning

As we walk through the gates of innocence
Our mentality risks new chances
Our bodies change in ways of trend
Our surroundings, a game with no end

We become labeled by our mentors
Our self-respect becomes selfish, wanting more
Chances limited to certain kinds
Though words of disgrace become hidden lies

Our image carried to what's been followed
The souls become open and hearts become hollow
Our eyes become blinded to our heart's physical needs
The air becomes sour with skies that bleed

Time is shortened, the stakes are high
The knowledge taught left by our guide
For we walk the path of split decisions
A strong sense kept with one expression

Lyrics are heard and spoken wise
The image portrayed cracked the broken cries
Our innocence is no longer of existence
Mentally speaking, we've reached the distance.

By: Giulia Ricciardi
August 28, 1995

Surviving the Game

Racing with the beat of the tribe
For pain is the forgotten eye
Drifting down this sea of red
Surviving the game, protecting the dead

Rapid ties, ridged paths and chanting cries
The thought to reach common ground alive
For mystic words and ancient stones
Clouded hope, tired hands and broken bones

Nothing's left in this heart's domain
A soul that drifts through the poisoned rain
The mind inside with sounds that weep
The eagle's cry, the voice that speaks

A destined dream shall never be seen
What left ahead the wounds that bleed
Followed myths and chanting rhymes
Calms the curse of the golden eyes

The garden ahead is my one escape
Where the souls are transferred to another fate
There I shall be left in peace again
A spirit lifted to the garden's domain.

By: Giulia Ricciardi
April 1, 1996

The Follower

He walks alone the city streets
Trying to escape the bloody mess
The only sound he hears, his heartbeat
Hoping to find a place to rest
As he gazes at himself what does he see
A young boy with a gun that bleeds

Thinking back to how this all started
He was dope, hyped and cold-hearted
Didn't care for people's thoughts
Only remembers what he's taught
To him, family is the gun, as for the others
Who cares, it's all about his brothers

There are no more sunny days for him
For he's hung his life out on a limb
The forbidden lies, the hidden cries
He's conquered fear, what does he really feel
Why must he follow the life of his friends
When they all die in the end

Someday we will learn what we hold
The future lies in our hands, our dreams, our goals
For the decisions we make are not always good
Sets a lesson away from the hood
A true person can be unleased
So, I keep praying on, I keep the peace.

By: Giulia Ricciardi
July 29, 1993

Hope

Without a fear, you are strong
Positive thinking all day long
Counting the days 'til your time is done
Waiting to see the daylight come

The sleepiness nights, the feared sights
The soundless pain, the hope to stay sane
But you don't cry, don't shed a tear
Cuz you know, it will soon disappear

You suffered the consequences, paid for mistakes
For the future is left to concentrate
Looking forward to brighter days
Hope to terminate the old ways

So, go ahead, release your hate
Let it go and separate
All you need is the hope within your heart
For it is strong and will never part.

By: Giulia Ricciardi
November 9, 1993

True Forgiveness

Sometimes we feel so alone
Stranded and hurt with no one to hold
Surrounded by hate and torn apart
Don't they know you have a heart?

They look at you and call you names
Who are they when they caused the pain?
For they had made mistakes before
It never stopped you from loving them more

You have someone who believes in you
Who will sit and listen to your blues?
Who will give you a chance for a new life?
And leave all the bad memories behind

So, stop feeling neglected and alone
Stranded and hurt with no one to hold
For I am here and always will be
I will love you for all eternity.

By: Giulia Ricciardi
November 21, 1993

Avail the Soul

As a cold shiver flows through my body
A white silhouette appears before me
A soft whisper escapes the soul
With words of despair I cannot unfold

I reach out with my arms open wide
The pain is deep with hurtful cries
I cannot grasp for it's not mortal
But stand aside as its message is crucial

Releasing in soft whispers in melody
Informing me my heart holds a key
To release the pain and hurtful cries
To escape the loneliness that it binds

"There will come a time to acknowledge
The peace and harmony to which you pledge
But before I accept such a request
Conquer the evil hovering me, put it to rest"

Left in confusion to what's been told
The key to freedom for I will hold
Conquer the evil which harmed the wrong
A task I'll honour, it could do no harm.

By: Giulia Ricciardi
April 25 1994

Visual Thoughts

Tainted lies, burning words
Darkened nights, closed doors
Caught in chains, whispered sounds
Blowing winds, shooting sounds

Headed down this path of choice
Merry-go-round whispered voice
Thoughts are made, lust of blood
Floating down, reddish flood

Self destruction in the mind
Breaking up thoughts in time
Lost and found what I've owned
Twisted rage, deep in cold

Wheels of time sounds of tremor
Colours of night held to remember
Liquid air, shades of light
Musical vibes, fame to fight

Caught between an ego's trip
Words to curse, born to lip
Names to twist, hopes to break
Bodies in all, choices to make.

By: Giulia Ricciardi
July 25, 1995

Scrambled

Let me sing a song, let me chant a tune
Hold me close, hear my whisper, let it bloom
Searching for what has been lost
Melting the heart which has turned to frost

How come I hide behind these walls?
All expressions which are felt by all
I reason, I believe is I speak in words that grieve
Trying to lay my ground, set my creed

For words are broken, they may mislead
The passion is driven to set its needs
You feel the pain, sense its reason
Racing through time, change of seasons

These patterns collide, pictured confusion
And what's left is life's disillusion
Forcing the ground, I walk on not to break
My life's adventure is left at stake

Scrambled, I will not fall, hit the surface
I may be fragile, my smile leads my purpose
I've left my mark in this world of hate
A journey hasn't ended; there's more to make.

By: Giulia Ricciardi
June 2004

Sun Embraced

Searching for an unforbidden sanctuary
Where images, liquidized, entertained lazy
Skies tainted statues lit with comfort
This expression enlightened its solid heart

Enhanced a light, given a warm embrace
Follow its breeze beyond the touch of faith
A place where thoughts considered left controlled
This comfort zone shimmers in gold

Time always exceeds its turn of hands
Melted, it becomes seeded by land
A growth shown by an honor listed
For only its dreams become simplicid

I yearn a passion, I released its lust
Received a pain beyond a given thirst
Only scars surface, for love is lost
A darkness hovers this kiss of frost

Find its comfort zone, set its peace
Give a love, persuade a poisoned feast
Enhance a passion, forgetting its history
Let the lust linger in simplicity

Touch this heart, tender as its skin
Find its yearning, clean its sins
Embrace its touch find its home
Free this soul, life its stones.

By: Giulia Ricciardi
April 2001

The Fighter

There always seems to be a little story to tell
Of dreams and visions for this girl gone to hell
For it starts out with courage and devotion
Just to get lost in the state of its confusion
Everything to her has become so clustered
Her mind is pulled towards clouds so dusted

She spirals in a fallen faith of truth and beliefs
And all she finds is the thirst of jealous thieves
How to focus her mind with all its confusion
Everything dropped in her path becomes an illusion
Pushing through roadblocks destined to succeed
In silence her hurt builds up, left with fallen tears

The one thing she yearns for is the thing holding her back
The purest of love to be found, the chaos it tracks
No matter the direction taken, she foregoes the outcome
Of a broken heart and alone for what's been done
In the dark she prays for a brighter light to appear
The distance ahead seems to be the mission in fear

As she falls more than one could count and record
She picks herself up and releases the given cord
Determination will not falter her, as she is strong
She's gone through too much to turn back now, hold on
Proceeding with strength pushing fear aside
The road ahead will break to a destiny with pride

She is a fighter, this one who breaks on through such hate
Down the paths of rocky roads and a destructive fate
The prize of success may come with few defeats
For no sacrifice in life comes with the rewards to reap
Hands of time will always turn, balance the expectation
Then she will rise to all she has accomplished in her direction.

By: Giulia Ricciardi
March 2005

Shine

Powdered grounds, rugged edges
　Dirty skies and sweet revenges
Distant voices heard from within
Frightened cries are kept hidden

The murky waters, the cold rain
The tears disguised behind the pain
The blood that drips from the wounded scar
The distant walk towards the evening star

As the night shivers the souls are barred
The spruce's coat becomes my guard
Nature's cry guides my sight
Counting on the morning light

The willowed path, the rocks engraved
The unknown challenged left unscathed
As the river's soft sounds guide my way
The owl's hoot calms until the morning's day.

By: Giulia Ricciardi
September 1995

Forgive and Forget

I reminisce of the time you were around
When things were simple, kept in sound
When there was nothing much to prove
To gaze upon my thoughts of you

Captured life's moment in time
Freeze control, the hands of time
Setting our fates of the destined path
Diminishing the thought of the haunted past

I would bless above to keep me strong
And situate my place to belong
In your world to rest in peace
Diminishing the thought of intended feast

A no-end situation forgetting its surroundings
Left with the unexplained endings
Life's simple facts have concluded with me
Thinking back to how it used to be

Though the memories are left to reflect
As sometimes it is best to forget
To look beyond the promise given
Once again, the past is left hidden.

By: Giulia Ricciardi
July 17, 1997

Plantation of Pain

Though a shadow may pass through broken fields
A spell will cast for promised fields
To pressure and prey against the ones who hurt
To attack and rebut the wicked curse

To thrive off power for leader's role
To deepen the pain of the darkened soul
For who am I to speak my heart
When the wicked curse sheds my part

I shall sweep the dust that lays on the grounds
And turn my head to the cursed rounds
For I am that person who speaks her thoughts
The precious soul whose lyrics shall rot

For they who fight for leadership role
Who grasp and take, who lust for more
They neglect the arms of time
The souls which enter this world confined

Well, the facts are laid to place of fame
Where greed is lust and pain is game
The thirst of blood is what they crave
For they will fall to their shallow grave.

By: Giulia Ricciardi
September 22, 1995

Elements of Life

Lost my heart, lost my mind
Its drive a thrust with no guidance
A destiny scattered, endless in time
And its pattern built in fences

The path to exit is left forbidden
As the paths ahead are poisoned red
To conquer, find the sacred door hidden
Only then you shall escape the common thread

To hide, to run, not to say a word
Becomes a balance out of control
Can't fight its fate, can't defend what's heard
For such of life has taken its toll

Instead, express, unleash its infliction
A heart which deprives the mind
Then let it become the cured infection
Conquer the red held in time.

By Giulia Ricciardi
May 2001

Beyond Misery

What makes the flame that burns the light?
What takes the pain that causes the fights?
Deceived by greed, obsession of love
Or hatred grown of past lives we shove

How do you hide the shame that's carved?
How do you remove the painful scars?
What does it take to vanish the mind?
I'll tell you my sacred cries

The dreadful screams, the shattered lies
The dripping tears, the swollen eyes
The flash of colours painted death
The hours after the deserted mess

Prayed for glory, yet raised in darkness
Evil has damned its place to rest
Captured in a world of beasts
With no escape of the destined peace.

By: Giulia Ricciardi
July 17, 1995

Lost Compassion

Beautiful, you are spared to believe
Each lyric spoken plants a seed
Fallen sacrifices yearning for release
Limits the time loving to please

Envisioned a thought beyond the years
For I had to have felt the lover's plea
I loved, I've touched passions desire
Our hearts yearned, torched its fire

I dance in circles, rhyme in chimes
A fool's heart to believe the given lies
My world has fallen, crept in sorrow
Not laced in glamour, nor essence of gold

Every turn disguised in masks
Unconditional love becomes the task
The flames that were, are ashes drifted
Trying to evolve, my soul now has lifted.

By: Giulia Ricciardi
November 10, 1998

Absence

To open our mind, look into my eyes
To split apart from truth to lies
To unleash your emotions, this I'm sure
Break the chains, find the cure

A face we try never to forget, we say
What do we know, it's now a new day?
To wander upon this broken path
Always a reminder of our darkened past

Shattered thoughts with bright lights
Left forgotten in these brutal nights
Spun by time, driven by the heart
Full of emotions, waiting to part

All I can say is I give you my heart to bear
For its destiny that will shed this soul to spare
You must seek and stop the mind from turning
It will take you in to the deep, left burning.

By: Giulia Ricciardi
March 1995

Released

Alas, a deep sleep has overcome my soul
Sweat and tears was not my goal
Visions are built beyond its kind
Its destination defies my mind

Soft whispers of your voice, lasting impression
Hover my body, wrapping in expression
Heat off your flesh inflates my blood
Like a daggered spear, drifts and floods

Beautiful you are, left an inscription carved
For your embrace is felt from afar
Though frozen I've become, your passion I lust
Bound and tombed, blessed by trust

Darkness has become light, breaking the mould
The poison once casted purified as gold
The fear repressed stands on guard
Its treasure is sacred, protected and barred

Refined a captured moment may rise
Give this love, torch this heart, uncast all ties
Give this courage, show me passion, bless my release
A soft melody shall rise giving me peace.

By: Giulia Ricciardi
June 1998

Images

Blue clouds form into rain clouds
Raindrops splatter on the ground
Spin around and watch me fly
Lost in time, feeling high

Colours flashing in my mind
As I'm lost, shattered in time
Shadows haunting, voices whisper
Eyes so tainted and dazed, just watch her

Nothing stands, nothing's real
Break my trip, my fist you'll feel
Dazed and confused, I'm lost in my thoughts
Conversation is wise, hit the right spot

I gander upon what's in my sights
Bodies around, take on the night
To catch and keep is the task
Go wild, enjoy it, if it lasts.

By: Giulia Ricciardi
September 1994

A Wilderness Cry

The water flows down the stream of gold
Its destination nobody knows
Its speed picks up faster and faster
Follow it through the forest's pasture

The birds chirp the cricket's melody
The trees sway as the wind picks up slowly
The sun sets beneath the clouds
The night is left with sounds of wolves' howl

A light fog begins to hover the land
The leaves fall strand by strand
The sky has darkened of many shades
The moon shines bright as it never fades

The forest has come alive
The sound of music nature's cry
A sacred land with a voice so strong
So why must man do the wrong?

By: Giulia Ricciardi
August 1, 1993

Solider Within

Rising through present and future
Unaware of the emotions given, felt pure
To believe is the fault that's held
When dreams are given a pledge

Its control felt, its matter sought out
For the mind is what sets its doubt
A reflection shown, our test of life
As theory helps understands our desire

For the scale's way itself
Its definition absorbed and felt
Answers known to man, unrealistic
Each thought given is exquisite

Absorb your surroundings, feel your soul
A life given short never untold
Survival we learn with given opinions
For the man alone will find solutions

All we strived, lived and learned
Knowing what's right, we pass aside to burn
In the end separated on self-image
Leaves our courage a bit damaged

Define yourself, absorb mind, body and soul
Only thoughts pure to oneself can unfold
Your definition for all images frowned upon
Will unleash the power felt, mankind stays strong.

By: Giulia Ricciardi
August 24, 2001

Exodus

Haunted by broken memories
Running from the found conclusions
Distant in mind, dazed by fantasy
Life which passes, portrayed an illusion

The days lost, the nights vanished
My spirit tainted, my body poisoned
The hidden pain has unleashed
The stage of denial has ended

My self image has shattered red
My heart has turned stone cold
Existing beyond the dead
Where the moon and stars considered gold

Tantalized by its vision
Excepted, a place with no restrictions
Pleased to my desires my decisions
Master for my actions

Liquid air, mystic ties and symbolic ores
A freak of nature is a world so twisted
An obsession has aspired more, for
My existence here has become unlisted.

By: Giulia Ricciardi
August 25, 1995

Consumed

I hide a picture in a perfect place
Its descriptor is freedom of face
To wander, to learn, our knowledge expressed
For who will listen, visions repressed

To paint this portrait of purity
Lashes out its individuality
Lost in expression, I give you peace
Understanding life fulfill its needs

Feel my pain, a lust I desire
A pureness I'm feeling, a sense of fire
Though poisoned with life's expectancy
Followed by the hurting of its discrepancy

My thirst for danger followed by adventure
My thoughts of hate lured to the future
What lies beneath, the purity of demise
The darkest depth of truth and lies

Guide my soul and free its mind
Unleash this fascination, bind the tide
Though individual expression left forbidden
Given its time, leave it hidden

A spirit invoked by compassion
A kiss shall break this dark fixation
So far beyond the time has past
A spinning dial consumed at last

Addicted towards a passion I trust
A shady image unleashed, fulfilled its lust
I leave a warning to all who patronize
Consumed, she bleeds, she shall hypnotize.

By: Giulia Ricciardi
March 1st, 2004

Departure

A sadness overcomes from the start
For you told me you had to part
Separate from the wickedness and confusion
To restore yourself, find a conclusion

Knowing there's no reason I may say
To keep you from going astray
For I wanted to explain and reveal my emotion
Now the years will pass without the notion

I cherish each moment that passes by
When we're together side by side
The touch of your hands will restore my warmth
The words you preached, the chance of hope

As the time nears, soon you must leave
Alone again with no one to reason
I will regret not telling you before
For you I need and felt much more

You never know, someday you'll return
We can rekindle this fire once burned
One thing I shall always remember
A friendship started, a friendship forever.

By: Giulia Ricciardi
April 18, 1994

Dedicated to J. Liston

Denial of Love

For every whisper that's been said
Every word has its bend
Fools unleash scattered thoughts
A battle in mind I have fought

For every horoscope is a verse
But it's reality, left a curse
Every lyric left forbidden
For the emotions felt, left hidden

The times have past beyond each thought
And the emotions buried within the spot
To unleash what's said to what's heard
To forget the pain, a lesson learned

For every child has its destined dream
For the path set can be secured, but can bleed
Though broken arrows may never be found
My heart in effort, left in bound

Sometimes visions appear through broken windows
The image portrayed a broken wishbone
For to wish upon what is cursed
To believe my heart will be left to burst

For never imagined this word called love
Never shall be, like the faded dove
But kept in mind my tired heart
The tears and pain received a place to part.

By: Giulia Ricciardi
November 1996

Exhausted in Thought

The need to be free, yet I am feeling lost
I'm finding myself, is a mission at cost
Though a direction we seek, boredom we find
A breaking point we have come to fall behind

Our mission is lost beyond our despair
A question we find imperfect and unfair
Perhaps our vision is broken, left unexplained
Then turned into memories faded in pain

Puzzled, we fall, finding its direction in peace
Though our answers conceived, what does it mean
So, our happy medium is left unbalanced
Undiscovered, it sets a pattern distanced

So why does this energy drown in my sorrows
Why is the humour left unleased to it trauma?
Exhausted is who I am, riddled in speech
For what's heard tends the soul to teach

Everything has become illustrated, it's nauseous
My visions may be clear, yet I'm exhausted
By its matter of meaning behind what's depicted
What happens to our world if it becomes evicted?

By: Giulia Ricciardi
August 2004

Justified

A hidden secret can become true to what's painted
For once it's released, try to become acquainted
For its clarification is misunderstood by some
To absorb its definition is to become undone

I believe to become in a controlled world of balance
The ones who fight its reason becomes a challenge
Not to say what's preached must be understood
It's reading between the lines, justify what's heard

Are we here for its knowledge or to be judged?
Is it the visual aspect we portray, how we pledge?
Toss our thoughts in a bottle and shake it about
Pop its cork, unleash its liquid, paint some notes

Well, I must believe it could all just be our fates
To understand, to what feeds our appetite, on plates
For I do believe in matters of truth left unspoken
Express it to all is the task at hand, becomes the token

We are all here, are we listening, a melody played
Tries to hide itself so softly, it mimics to be betrayed
Blurred we still become blind to what's disclosed
Our fault is our weakness, it's what's imposed

Pathetic our battles, we fight for a place of existence
Afraid, we doubt ourselves, to pursue the given distance
And none the less at times we may stand alone
We mould ourselves in truth, not cast the first stone.

By: Giulia Ricciardi
2006

Cast Away

Rivers of gold drift me away
Its destination two worlds astray
Voices in the air taint each image
This shady nightmare, a dream so strange

A spirit carries me, understanding its harmony
Unsure, my thoughts dizzy, left indignity
Is this heaven ahead or the core of my solutions?
For I feel this presence eludes its devotion

The running waters set me appease
My heart afraid and starts to weep
I can't find myself, for once lost in time
My length of journey unknown to mind

Images appear and go left in confusion
For your voice, your face guides my illusion
My tears flow like the given river
My screams unheard, I'm lost in shivers

Our worlds must collide, how can it be
For you are the night, I am the day in need
Start your journey, follow its seed given
Free your heart, beyond the forbidden

Cast your sail high, fly like wind
I am a treasure lost, I've lost its twin
For this mission a prize left to uncover
Shall redeem our souls carved forever.

By: Giulia Ricciardi
March 8, 2004

Emptiness

As I sit here alone
Sitting in my room so cold
I reminisce of those days
For it feels just like yesterday

Your voice your laughter, I feel no fear
Keeps me safe in those sleepiness nights
Why does it feel I'm chasing a dream?
I sense that your presence is near
How can I take this time to rest?
For all I feel is emptiness

This feeling is eating me up inside
No sure how I've kept it in disguise
Do I walk away and say goodbye?
Surrender myself to you and confide?

I know I must forget and move on
Deep inside I know we don't belong
You're still a part of me since we've parted
I will keep those memories deep within my heart.

By: Giulia Ricciardi
February 14, 1994

Imperious

You walk along with an image so cavalier
   Yet your impression given revealed
Your words you preach are brave, so you say
Yet you complicate and hesitate the prey

Your decisions must always be correct
Though your interpretation, left neglected
Your eyes stare and linger, though it's just a thought
Which seems genuine as you believe, just to taunt

Though I sit back and watch through it all
I find a true meaning in your expression to fall
You say one day I will learn and stand tall
When I've lived the same words, my call

Words are wisdom through its preacher
Yet your words have fallen, the given teacher
Speak to me with reason, maybe I'll return
Help me to understand, I'll find what's turned

Confusions of being, for all is left exceeding
Beyond my existence, finish what I'm succeeding
This may be what's left of a last impression
For I need to be understood, it's your discretion.

By: Giulia Ricciardi
July 2004

The Shining

Awaken to feeling of emptiness inside
Burning deep from the words left to confide
A fate set, your path left at stake
And the lyrics sung, defying in your fate
Your pride is what you preach
Though violence at hand left to teach
No bars, no chains to hold you down
But the image proceeds its destined ground

It's no lie, all eyes are on you
The young who foresee your words are true
A vengeance filled with hate and blood
In their eyes you're the god who fills the love
For yet you weep for each one's loss
But words in fault, whose image is boss
Right before your eyes are visions of black
Respect given for the ones who act

When does it end? What does it take?
A young heart with a trigger of hate
What lyrics are sung then? Who's to blame?
When the path followed is the rebellious fame
Its starts with what had been overturned
Which attracts its name and heads turn?
When the flame diminishes, becoming its spirit
Its soul will drift, never resting: that's your demerit
So, chant your lyrics, chant your cry
For you've sparked its flame, set your ties
Poisoned your own blood with darkness
Now you will earn the above respect.

By: Giulia Ricciardi
August 1997

The Watcher

Emptiness fills my soul with deep despair
For a part of me wishes you were still here
Who was to think they would take you away?
In little time spent, for you I pray

You lay so peaceful, so still and cold
You were warm and sweet, a heart of gold
A life so young with friends who cared
But now you're gone, left us in despair

The crows now follow my every lead
My views now darkened, my heart now bleeds
Darkness hovers and I feel alone
Your voice I hear with a humorous tone

Whispers are heard from all around
You're buried now, six feet in the ground
Your soul has lifted, and I feel your presence
I must move on, time is of the essence

You will drift along and watch over me
For the emptiness is gone, your warmth I feel
The sky has parted and daylight breaks
A crow still follows me, every step I take

He will guard my path and help me understand
The concept of life's coming demands
He is your soul with a heart of gold
As my saddened heart shall mend to mould.

By: Giulia Ricciardi
November 8, 1994
In memory of Timothy W. Stevenson

Twin Soldiers

Sometimes pressure can fly spread its demise
Like it's deepened despair, you keep its high
Finding its soul expresses new meaning
Given the acceptance to what's pleasing

Absorbed, we've now become spontaneous
To become released, my energy becomes relentless
To follow this path may restore some loss
To express it represses the dark if crossed

Your spirit guides my soul, left mesmerized
For it's delayed my time, you're so dignified
Breathless left with a heart that shines
Withdrawn must I be; for the hands of time

Passionate by words of action, triumphant by all
You are soldiers by extremist, determined by gull
For your domain is left calm at ease
Though your charm feeds off a given need

Unpredictable, your world becomes absorbed
For I am no longer withdrawn, but climb aboard
A friendship in destination always left unknown
Soldiers armoured protected the spirit and soul

Believing is to understand every saga continues
For those who survived, left are few
No matter the consequences, a solider brave
The story told, once lost now saved.

By: Giulia Ricciardi
March 2004

Memory Lane

The music kicks its melody
 Soft sounds, drums beat heavily
Crazed emotions skimmer through my mind
Damn I'm running out of time
Run, run I say
Run, run before it goes away
Scurry through the fields of joy
Feeling like a little boy
Flowers blooming in the grass
Now its time to forget the past
Looking towards a brighter day
What more must I say
People hurt, People cry
People hate, People lie
I trust my soul in my hands
None else seems to understand
One day I shall escape this world of hate
And drift off to a better place
So, hear me out, hear me loud
I've drifted off into the clouds.

By: Giulia Ricciardi
August 3, 1993

Puzzled in Time

Erase the time given, yet so implicated
The race, the burn set is exquisite
Your face an image beyond its picture
For its spirit left beyond is pure

Who am I left, with a reflection?
The individual scarred beyond rejection
For I yearn a burning lost sensation
And your world has poisoned its temptation

I turn, I run with no direction
Yet to foresee the given intention
As images portray the youth inside
My eyes burning by its set demise

A friendship, a bond broken, shattered
The why is asked, my heart matters
I break, I fall, I bleed impulsive
For they shall follow, become decisive

Sense to make through given drafts
Yet to unleash regrets is the backlash
A puzzle, maybe, a Rubik's cube
Each individual left alludes

Find me, unleash this demon inside
Relinquish its purity, for each life is pride
A finding has uncovered the words decrypted
One time the hand shall free its life listed.

By: Giulia Ricciardi
March 1 2004

My Hero Envisioned

There's a certain affection that I've been fighting
For the uncertainties are beyond feeling slighting
With so much to lose, the risk of satisfaction
The words and whispers go beyond the attraction
I've pushed away such feelings, been self-destructive
Such a thrill inside, it just exits what's driven
For my battles have become such stories enlisted
Just try to envision such drastic decisions persisted

When comes the time for this to come to its end
Proceeding through like a game, just to pretend
Such hardship that falls apart, built up into fear
To balance justice, throughout the fallen years
Thinking at night the sense of charm and laughter
Just keep pushing on to this constant battle
You are the reason for happiness in my life
What keeps me together, what keeps me alive

You have given a friendship that I cherish in life
I would give anything to have you, in this time
I'm helpless and just want to run in your direction
The constant thought of feeling your affection
Your bright eyes, your soft lips, your beautiful face
Such strong arms, that feeling of your strong embrace
To hide such emotions from reality is what I hate
The reasons given just to protect our given fates

When I look at you, I foresee what lies for us ahead
All these emotions become unleashed, lying in bed
A hesitation prevents me from reaching towards you
The facts are what matter it's written in scripture
A cycle to be revealed, just take that step, be brave
Just go with the flow as destiny can be an enclave
So, if these images and thought can become true
It has become so clear I'm destined to be with you.

By Giulia Ricciardi
April 2006

In Control

It's funny how our mission is not what we expect
Becomes the unexpected, gives us more to reflect
What we have is what's left neglected
But more so to our hearts becomes defective

We know where the path leads, refuse the belief
It makes us known to all our shadows, given thieves
Known not to admit, only to deny and lead
Yet like flowers we plant our blessed seeds

For I may sit and ponder to all that I want
Yet I know I set temptation to which it taunts
My thoughts are consistent in which they haunt
Which poisons the mind, turns our veins in knots?

The need to separate like vinegar and oil has its toll
Like our lives, we become convinced, stay in control
And sure enough, the pain becomes the stories told
It's how we accept our demise to stand strong and bold

Always the chance to fall, yet not ready to fail
Mistakes are a given it's the conclusion to hail
On top we need to stand to tell its given tale
Our visions become the marriage, our beautiful veil

Do I sense defeat in the life ahead that's given?
Or do I endure the possible negative that's hidden
The muse does not ponder such restrictions
Failure is not the possible way to expectations.

By: Giulia Ricciardi

Unpredictable

I find this vision, it's all I see
I feel its purpose, I find its being
I second guess, I sense each doubt
For I never forget my vision in thought

I scatter, I rush, I absorb each presence
Then I believe this is my existence
To understand is the mission I carry
To all who believe is the task left in worry

So how to escape this destination
If all that's left is the chaos enlisted
To convince is beyond my reach
How to set a stand, whom to preach

Words are spoken everyday for knowledge
Now all who lead manipulate and pledge
Boundaries and rules powered by reaction
And the given laws left to its own actions

Difficulty exceeds in all our decisions
So why create and absorb its illusion
Our existence is to find a happy medium
To resist becomes part of all our intentions

Then here's a thought to all in belief
I am being surrounded by deceit
So I may react, may not be understandable
That's what makes our life so unpredictable.

By: Giulia Ricciardi
March 2005

No Strings Tonight

So, I have a thought or two for you, or maybe a gesture
It might be something of interest to you this I'm sure
More towards the move of a set game of pleasure
That's if your down with that type of endeavor
An energy inside my body that wants to unleash
A moment I wish to share, to release beyond belief

It can, for a moment set aside or forbidden fears
A mission in control setting the ride in full gear
A one-time invitation for you, my secret V.I.P
Behold, you can be sure to keep your trust in me
Start with simple martinis, your taste for pleasing
Whatever your pleasure, just follow my lead

The night is young, let the music set you free
All I need is a moment of your time, you will see
Drink your Bacardi, relax your mind, loosen up
Take my hand and join the party, just one touch
Come and play with me, I'm eyeing those lips
My temperature is rising, my thirst for your kiss

You can get to know me, or do you prefer a mystery
I'll unwind to candle light and my martini pickled sweet
Come play with me, my body moves to the music's melody
Set expectations aside, I'm expressing what is real
Step inside my domain, and just set yourself free
We can spice things up, whatever suits your fantasy

A simple thought of pleasure I want to explore
No time to hesitate, what are we waiting for?
I'm not here to envision with words of pressure
Just wanting to share my world of pleasure
For you give this girl a sense of adventure
Have you piqued an interest? Close that door.

Giulia Ricciardi

My Gladiator

If lyrics lure through spirit of song, it's true
The music can alter minds and talk to you
Than every word portrayed lands itself a place
For each word spoken drives away leaders of hate

For each lyric is a meaning, for its written
To decipher what I portray is the task hidden
Lead to be scars for the object of expression
Advanced in feelings, I'm left to drown in depression

Guidance is usually founded by its leader
The realism then becomes the true believer
A found spirit which falls and drifts in liberty
Absorbs its guidance so propounding, its destiny

My lyrics become surrounded, lured by pain
Drowning, I'm flooded by tears of rain
Rushed, inhibited, it's become an emotion undone
Except its purity has been poisoned for it has begun

The rhythm set drives the stake through the heart
This unexplained destination drives it apart
For every word to be found finds its melody
You have become my passion, my liberty

My lyrics become a contagion fascinated by destiny
Will it humiliate or free my existence to its purity
Find myself, my soul a melody in the distance
This is my world which enlightens my self-existence.

By: Giulia Ricciardi
May 24, 2004

Say Nothing

Why is it everyone has so much to say about nothing?
Yet I still try to hold back as retaliation is about something
Not the fear that may try to overwhelm, in control
Maybe it's time to just tell all the stories being told

I listen to thought, I listen to all its given reasons
But I still find it's blah, blah, blah, change the season
I blame myself at times, for the head just doesn't believe
It gets to a point where as I just want to heave

As it's knowing I can take in to all I am seeing
As I also know the hand that holds the maker's tyranny
I can place this all into one simple melody for you
It's like a rush that comes to my head, yes, it's true

So, I count the sheep in my head as I sleep cozy in bed
One sheep, two sheep, three sheep, let's just jump ahead
I awake for I haven't lost sleep, it's a reality I can't explain
One minute I'm here as for the next well, my story of fame

I riddle in words I can set a harmony, it's what I do
To ask of me to play a simple melody, just not the shoe
I take spoken words and spin it around to understand
The best of times I like to escape to the unknown land

So, for all the ones who have lots to say about nothing
To preach such distasteful words strum along and sing
This tune I will lay it out for you, pick a different note
Take your business elsewhere, truck a goat. 😉

By: Giulia Ricciardi

Implicated

Violated and stripped, left so implicated, you came
  Set my world apart, left your mark to believe, no games
You made cease to belief in love, my belief in life
Opened the doors of closure from your love
With my body left trembling, sense of nervousness
A part of being broken, chains of helplessness

In discretion left a pattern so implicated, left knowing
The one who chooses to linger is the one drowning
For even the lost must be found, giving its crowning
Turns the wheels, burns away for what's hiding
Finding its loop, set it astray, every bend unwinds
Leading to some destined happy ending, no more cries

I pray no tears are left to fall, left to bear or shatter
For it causes this flood, becomes its matter
You reach out, guide me to the driest of lands I see
Yet an emptiness still lingers, it follows me
No paper news, yet no comic strips are here to view
The images left behind are just faded of you

Violated, stripped left so implicated you came
Like my morning coffee, slice of pie, no blame
Created a vision so deep, I'm left in confusion
The cards dealt are paved for my restitution
And the morning's sunshine, the lyrics don't lie
You have left me unhinged to this story implied.

By: Giulia Ricciardi
June 2004

Consumed in Fear

As fear builds up inside me, I become absorbed
The thought of hurt leaves me disturbed
Mistakes are made in constant motion
Exhausted over time, searching for a notion

A pattern scattered I fear to express
As time becomes such a consistent test
It pulls away from my greatest expression
Though leaving a mark of a lasting impression

Sometimes fear can persist and misguide
Will to exist can be fatal to our pride
I wish to have faith and evade the soul
I have become weak to achieve the goal

In search for the one I adore, I keep sacred
Only to lose the faith it may never unfold
Maybe skeletons buried have unleashed
In pieces they come to reckon a peace

My ghost, my guardian, a solider in place
The spirit is felt near, I heed its fate
Its driven presence has turned my thoughts
I've become lost in a world which haunts

There is a gift that has touched my spirits
The words become expression in lyrics
Can it be fear, a chance to present itself
To guide my existence, to be at my best.

By: Giulia Ricciardi
March 2005

The Preacher

Just make it stop, that sound of hate
The constant hurt of being lost and betrayed
A blessed harmony, what it's trying to portray
As it draws its beauty in, as it hunts its prey

There lies a mission I can only guide
My knowledge is profound, it finds its light
It feeds adventure forced by pride
It takes my being, it's what gives me drive

For battles ahead will always have barriers
It may hold us back, it turns us into terrors
We then become soldiers so disillusioned
Searching that key to freedom of confusion

The story becomes the lead, we are human
The energy pushes us to drive our conclusion
Engaged, we wish to be heard beyond our beliefs
To be part of that voice whose words will set free

We are bound to preach the truth that's given
Words of knowledge that are kept hidden
Visions absorbed, secrets become the least
Acceptance of one's self becomes the priest

I have the wisdom inside, I fight with courage
To spread, as others refusal to nourish
The minds have become weak, so self-absorbed
A definition in the reliance behind that closed door.

By: Giulia Ricciardi

Can You Hear Me?

I've been up, I've been down, I've been lost, I've been found
I have been to the point of no return, can you hear me, I'm bound
Yet I seem to always break free trying to understand
Why does this seem to be the repeat of my fight to stand
Can you hear me, when do I get my happy ending, my turn?
I look around and hear the whispers, I feel the burn

To the bottom, to the top, I have grasp on to know
It always seems to be an episode of the same show
So much has been given, yet a lot has been lost
To see in return, I'm in recovery to pining a loss
So, when does it give in? Just please tell me
This chaos is a curse that seems to surround me

It's hard for me to breathe, like a constant hiccup
Can they hear me? It just keeps blowing up
Looking for that place of peace, seems like forever
Just want to disappear from this chaos of love I endeavor
Back to the beginning again, try to come up with a plan
Something's got to give for this is not who I am

Its like I'm writing a script to my own movie
My cast is hard, lost in a twisted fate of its reality
Searching to find someone out there just like me
Holding on to that happy ending I truly believe
Skip to the part where she finds her mate
To only find out it's a disaster carving her fate

Can you hear me? Can you catch my plea?
Is this just becoming my reality, is it just a dream?
My heart is turning cold here, can anyone hear me?
Turning into this goddess of dark can you release me?
Can't even sleep in peace as these nightmares haunt me
My mind in a painted motion of its questioned reality

By: Giulia Ricciardi

This Planet We Grow

Danger becomes the revenge we wish to release
Our spirit becomes torn apart, wanting to unleash
We think life is so perfect, yet we all have dreams
We sit here so pompous in clarity, set to believe
We hide, we lie, heck, we deceive in our given pride
No room left for change as we bathe in a pool of lies

It just seems strange to me, we've become oblivious
Has it really come down to our mental state so clueless?
For intelligence comes with given knowledge, I guess
Respect comes with ownership, this I contest
The lore becomes our honour for that's what's pledged
Well, in this sort of relationship, I do truly dread

We're supposed to find balance in this planet we ignore
Water flows around us until the calm hits the storm
Then the air becomes poisoned with power of destruction
Until somebody tries to place a guide of restrictions
And fires will burn until there's nothing but ashes
Common sense does not comprehend to a bunch of asses

Then the world becomes a canvas, a picture left painted
Stuck in a rhythm of confusion, loss and despair, tainted
Explosive and ready to erupt down below, our cities fall
Then the finger gets pointed to who dropped the ball
It's becoming a constant joke, no time to be so serious
Until its poison runs in our rivers, then we become furious

But who am I, for no one listens to me in the best of times
They all ask for help then turn it around, it stands and binds
I have no power, no bolts of lighting to thrown down
That sparks that fire under these asses and clowns
I can only sit back and watch this world spin in chaos
I can bitch and preach but to them I am a lost cause.

By: Giulia Ricciardi

Balanced

Sometimes our test in life becomes challenged
And not only does it lose your balance
But it lays the doubt, poisoned by thought
Must be the knowledge what's left to be taught

There are beliefs which drive our being
Now how does one escape a mind in planning
It's our own society that balances our tendencies
Sad to say we've trailed to become legendary

Surprised to see the world of greed
How it sucks the poison, refills the need
A hate in desire has carried its being
The blind eye has turned to what's needing

We hate to give, regret to ask: a truth hidden
Have we become absorbed: are we forsaken?
Cursed we turn and reject our passion
The negative fear has buried such compassion

Such hate to give our self-resemblance
Does this replenish the given resistance?
Cowards we become, sucked away by fear
Inside we die of the internal need

One day shall come and awaken the soul
By then we're absorbed, becoming the fool
Shall not lose faith, shall not forget
This is my life, a mark in test .

By: Giulia Ricciardi
2006

Coloured in Sin

I see an enchanting path which I'm running
Secrets and lies, demise of the corruption burning
Wanting to just break off and release what's inside
Wanting to release who I am, for this I cannot hide

Finding my truth, always treading waters
I am drowning in my sorrows, stripping in desire
My secrets in heart scream to unleash
Find me, unleash me, who am I, can you see?

For my thirst for wine turns its colour ruby
Violated in sin, I'm battling, my stomach turning
Screaming in strength, my habits yet broken
You're suffocating my being, that door I must open

Part my walls, colour them in forbidden lies
Sparkle them true in colour, my creed I can't find
Break my silence, find me, create your shell
Paint these broken walls of colour, find its mend

What I've become, what has turned to curse
This person inside me, to what I have nursed
Fallen, I have become strong, I stand liquid in tears
Yet again, here I am in fear, yet again I can truly see.

By: Giulia Ricciardi
June 2004

Complicated

I must admit I'm not too sure what you expected from me
All the pressure I had, it created the beast in me
I suppressed it all inside, hiding in my humour you see
A constant mistake on my part, you had no faith in me
I find myself compelled to be this creator of peace
Though I'm numb, feeling helpless, help me, please

You portray an image, a picture I just can't paint
The ink is running thin on this one, just a big mistake
For like your lies I feel manipulated, yet no one listened
But thanks to the ones who all had participated
Guess your actions, your words, were the charm pretending
So much for you all, it was the harm that was intended

You had me so drawn in and yet made things so complicated
You had me set in your world, yet I still feel like I was baited
Its easy to let me go and go our separate ways at best
This thing between us has been such an awful mess
Even though it hurts to have to let things go, that's for sure
I'm better off to set a new venture, find what's pure

Patterns aren't meant to be broken, why did you break me?
Why did you pick me? My life was already a broken tragedy
Now everything is shattered, you've crushed its simplicity
Wickedness will find you one day, it may sound crazy
Followed in position, my place was a target set so easy
Yet you forget the hurt just fuels my drive, one day you'll see.

By: Giulia Ricciardi
May 2007

Fighting Battles

People hurting with words, trying to manipulate, hiding
Consequences known, yet still denying
So we stop just to see
They are not just hurting us can't you see
Is this just because we can't seem to believe
(I wonder, just wonder)

We all seem to just to get situated
Sometimes our own living becomes what's hated
We stop, take a chance
Not to return, make our stance
Then we see what's all around us
People dying, war at a plus
What becomes the answer, as power sees fit?
Twist the media as we become to realize this is bullshit

This is not our battle that were fighting, yet

People hurting and now we're trying
To make difference, some still hiding
It's not enough to see
Doesn't matter what we grow to believe
To fight against the power for money feeds
Industries are dying, practice what you preach
Just turning the other cheek

So how do you fight, it's government, just shout
How do disregard them and get your message out
Tired of all the people dying
Sick of seeing all this fighting
Want to live and breed in peace
Raise our children protect our world, please
If the love has gone then there's no hope left
I seem to believe there's no denying, we can't pretend

This is not our battle that we're fighting, yet

We rise above, justify what we fight for
We strive to believe there still is hope around that corner
We take our stand in hopes to be heard
Yet the cause is real emotions is a blur
Setting examples for the next generation
C'mon now, proceed with no hesitation.

By: Giulia Ricciardi
July 2014

On My Own

So here we go, pendulum swinging left to right
Years have passed as I still sit here alone in thought
Been a long-time pen to paper late at night
Yet life's a vicious circle, a sentence to dot

So, here we go yet again, the hints I've thrown
Not sure anyone can hear me, or see me in sight
Feeling like a stray dog, just throw me that bone
In the dark alone and cold such a common night

As I drown in my thoughts, waiting for more
I start to light a fire let that light shine through
I have stopped running, I've closed that door
My heart is warming up, yet patience not a virtue

I toss, I turn, can't sleep at night, visions that haunt
Love is what I once yearned for, now it's left to burn
Funny how once it's what I wished for, it launched
In some bad way, yet happy I took the time to learn

I guide my path, I can find myself through the dark
Constantly left on my own, dependant on myself
I have my self-love, I show my strength, do my part
I go beyond given hell, I've come to peace without help

Though I hate it to be said as a constant reminder
For separation has been the cost of a lost cause
I do not feel the concept of defeat that hinders
As I've learned it's a stepping stone, a round of applause

The avenue ahead doesn't seem all that bad, I see
A step at a time helps me understand the future
Just sometimes Its surrounded by its negativity
I am a wishful thinker, positivity dominates I'm sure.

By: Giulia Ricciardi
July 2015

A Feeling Repressed

You know, it's been a long time since I've come around
It's been a long time since I've lost my ground
I can turn to the left, I can turn to the right
I can feel out my best, this is my life
Nothing left in stopping me now
Won't let anyone come and stop me now

You have come about for a mission to become
Now I really have the chance, to express this love
You have made me feel, you have turned me around
You have allowed me to see, stand my ground
Now it's just so plain to see, a common reality
This is about you and me in a dream, my fantasy

For I hang on to every word that you said
I play it repeatedly, like a song in my head
It could only be what it's meant to be
In all respect it hits me fast and reveals
Its hard to forget such feelings inside, you see
But I must allow it to surface, I must believe

At times I feel drained just thinking about you
For nothing lasts forever, this is true
I can see your face every time I close my eyes
I can see how I it comes rushing like the tides
And though my heart pounds when I think of you
I know down the road I'll be seeing you.

By: Giulia Ricciardi

Lost Boy

Don't wanna hear your excuses
   Don't wanna hear your reasons
So, wrapped up in your set fuses
Wanting to feel about what pleases
I take the time trying to understand
Take that step back, what's the plan

I'm under this umbrella, looking up
To the skies above, don't give up
Wanting to run towards the night
My stomach's turning, why the fight
Hey, can you see me right now?
Can you look past this cloud?

Trying to clear my head, do what's right
I can't seem to find the reason, why fight?
Do you need this time to be alone?
Can you hear me, or is it just my tone?
Just seems to set you off when I speak
Like a water pipe about to spring a leak

You seem to be lost in sound, in the crowd
Gone in the past, can you hear me now?
How long will it last, what am I waiting for
This may take some time, closing the door
I'll be waiting here when the time has come
I'll be waiting for you when you are done.

By: Giulia Ricciardi

My Prayers to You

I've carried these thoughts and prayers, very few
Even though deep inside I've always known you
Through all the sadness, with the pain, the glory
I've always known your battles, your fate, your story
Even though the negative reflects the doubt
Your story has helped my own pain to fight
I have felt deceit, at times I have felt restrained
When in doubt your words comfort my pain

You're right when you lose yourself, fear of power
And battles one never forgets, defeat and conquer
Without saying a word your silence left an image
Scares me straight like the hatred in carnage
I can turn that pain, bring to a place of glory
Think of the laughter in a sweet place, a happy story
You can replace those hurtful memories hidden
To a place set beyond and forbidden

Where are you, my friend, I wish I could reach you
I can try to take that pain away, I shall comfort you
I'm sending out my prayers to you, can you hear me
I believe in hope, you have always had that, trust me
I can be your salvation, your temporary getaway
I wish not to burden, I need not a lengthy stay
Just to hold you for a moment make sure you're ok
Feel your sympathy of what's becoming, be on my way

For deep in your heart you may feel alone
Across the path you have my hand to hold
Unleash your thought, the words of the unkind
This I promised will help, release the bind
And we may never get that chance to seek
An opportunity to resolve such pain we keep
Faith one day will present a precious key
That will open that door and set its pain free.

By: Giulia Ricciardi

A Friendship Marked

Kindred spirit set in stone and shines
All who know him knows his kind
He walks a path in all directions
Grows in heart left with no perfection

Random ways, yet driven far from my task
Sometimes I wonder how he wears his mask
He felt so close to me, yet we were so apart
A bond I felt no matter the distant from the start

As time could stand, we led separate lives
He's become a father, perhaps grown over time
He had lived his life, yet foresees his gain
Time is short, plays a comfort in his pain

Unusual, yes this must be to keep this old friend
Once I believed we were friends to a lover's end
Guess the fate of chances from others he hurt
He just took for granted, oh, this I've learned

Sometimes, the fear of us to separate is our fate
But somehow it seems to be what's at stake
We have shared some laughs, we have heard our cries
No matter what someday we will share our times

Scarred hearts for we were two worlds apart
We have shared such moments from the start
Unforgiven he still believes in the love in me
For that I can cherish a friendship indeed.

By: Giulia Ricciardi

As You Are

It's funny how you are used to getting your way
Your likes, your dislikes, your feelings, it's okay
Then you go and throw a curveball my way
Not sure how to take it, such a disarray
Just not expected, I guess, what does it mean
It's your decision I'm sure, like rivers that stream
The constant flow of treading waters in the mist
State of confusion becoming such a pessimist

So many times, we become so blinded and confused
Fallen by broken decisions by what's abused
So how to divert in such orientated diversions
To prevent the worst expected, a bad conclusion
With shaken grounds that can become tectonic
The golden globe of our lives that become chaotic
We are souls fallen from grace to the unforbidden
We set our fates and unleash what's really hidden

Your ways are primitive, yet evolved you become
Dissecting the fear inside, banging on those drums
So how do you know when to separate your fate
You've become so absorbed, then linger to hesitate
When does it become out of your league?
For you stand ahead to strive and achieve
Careful, you are not to step on marked grounds
Analyzing each move, to this I have found

Knowing when to change, a tune meant to be
A good thing which happens, we must believe
Sometimes finding humour in our perspective
Defuses the explosion ready to be detected
Stranded, you are not alone, this story told
Rivers may run fast, as oceans vast and bold
As we are never stranded as at times you may feel
As things become your way, stand proud and achieve.

By: Giulia Ricciardi

Faded

I've been sitting here contemplating, beside myself
Trying to find a solution of truth to my hidden self
Can't imagine what this could do once expressed
But it's killing me inside just keeping this repressed
For there've been times I've been so illusive
And I can set off such an explosion of confusion

Repeated thoughts ponder, it comes and fades
Which has dug deep, sharp like jagged blades
For instinct takes over with a lot of doubt and fear
My indecision may lead to wounds that bleed
I know you're there, I can feel your existence
Just believe in me, I am feeling persistent

Have you ever had an expression felt inside?
Which makes your mind bleed, hearts collide
To expose oneself, but fear the release
You risk it all, left in failure and disbelief
With no control I am what's burning inside
It's given thirst alone that shakes my pride

I promised myself, convinced by my emotions
Once you've trained yourself it becomes a devotion
And each time a moment starts I fade away
Becoming that wall, with the visions portrayed
I'm feeling emptier as each day passes by
The closest to happiness, stretched beyond its time

So again, I'm drifted off to this world of lost
No one left to believe in, that given cost
No one left to hear my broken cries
No one to confront my existence or hidden ties
Just to feel completed is all that's wanted
All I ask, just come to me, it's what's granted.

By: Giulia Ricciardi
2006

This Ghost

I hear a sound, feel a scratch, sense its pleasantry
It disappears in character, reflecting its imagery
Its dark silhouette an image I can't portray
A spirit sought out, lost, left in disarray

Where are you now, for I can feel you
This ghost that haunts me, needs to peruse
As it's still in mourning, confused it may be
Deserted it seems, to capture, it eludes me

I'm still lost for words, understand its being
Confusion has lost your speech, regains its lead
An interruption explodes, a deception increased
The hurt surfaces beyond this spirit I see

From the cradle to its grave is what I'm fighting
No chance of the darkness to penetrate its lighting
You turn to illuminate the essence of pure
Your thirst to unleash a battle of the future

You become this hidden treasure of disguise
A path, a journey gone wrong, hurt by its demise
In your honour I will finish as per your request
Your light is calling, a journey you must lay to rest.

By: Giulia Ricciardi
2006

Suffocated

I've been around the ways, I've seen its magnitude
I've been pushed, I've danced around the truth
I can disguise the facts, become the drama's feed
But its purpose to challenge is what's believed
At first, we feel stripped to what we are given
Then retaliate in others, it's what's driven

For the consequences don't exist to them, no shame
They turn that blind eye like it's no fault, no blame
Technically just expected to take it on and listen
That sour taste that stains as its marked decisions
I've put myself out there, stretched out my being
Yet no matter how they dress it up it keeps feeding

Portraying a picture for all see its perfection
Living in lies and leaving all to be left restricted
Like a plague released, that swarms the city street
Drowning in poison of what's unleashed, we creep
I've come to think there is just no winning to this
Channeling the wrong, twisted in its bliss

All the top players have joined in this fruitful gain
My lungs feel heavy as my pours absorb the pain
Standing behind this sense of manipulation, I gasp
Finding an outlet to escape - where's my mask
Sickens me to see such distaste in a tangled weave
In the distance the fog is lifting, this I must believe.

By: Giulia Ricciardi

Voice of Reason

If there comes a time to say what I only knew
For all what I had to say, express it to please you
Would you stand by my side and hear me out?
Or would your walk away not care what its about
Perhaps it would comfort you take in your pride
Just look at it in a perspective, try not to just hide

I'm sure you've heard it all before, that same road
Where it never ends that twists and turns, you're floored
We all must face what's ahead for this I am sure
But it will become a relief to unleash it out, your cure
When you're down, it's guilt we look towards the blame
But there's hope there to see for this I feel your pain

We can sit here and analyze, it leaves no resolution
A constant banter back and forth, finding a solution
For it's what time is spent to fix the in-between felt
We all have problems here, wash it away, let it melt
For danger is part of the evils' displayed pattern
Like Alice and Wonderland with the Mad Hatter

Others seem to feed off what's become so tragic
Instead of stepping aside, taking that moment of logic
I can be that voice of reason and help with the burden
The trust in me needs to be the focus, are you listening?
I can't stand aside and watch the destruction of your being
Knowing a part of life is lead by the hand that's given

So, here's the thing, I can testify to your existence
I can guide you along, justify, become persistent
I can help change your thoughts, help with any decisions
If you become resilient and stand by its traditions
It could turn things around, be that voice of reason
For you've had it all along just ignored its sense of being.

By: Giulia Ricciardi

Changing the Game

Times I wonder I can't seem to figure this shit out
Feel like all are players, inside I want to scream and shout
Though I've been wrong before, more so always right
Suspicious it just seems to me to prove the fight
I'm sitting here not too far, music turned up in play
Dancing by myself, dancing the night away

Though my legs are burning, haven't rested today
As I listen to the words it takes my mind to a place
Where the hurt is gone, and the wind just blows
The sand between my feet, you know how it goes
No worries as our past is a drifted memory
A dream hazed over, going with the melody

I've tumbled over, I've fallen from grace at times
I've picked myself up, wiped the tears, cleared my mind
The tallest walls haven't stopped me, became persistent
People have hated my change from past existence
Can't handle what's been set in its prior state
For I've stopped counting on my given mistakes

I've come beyond these roads laid out in front of me
I've driven down the darkest of emotions, can't you see
I can lay it out so simple for them, still not recognizing
For Pete's sake, how is this just not registering?
I have learned not to let fear hold me back, its true
But it doesn't mean I don't care, I just don't value you.

By: Giulia Ricciardi

Karma

Sitting here in my messed up thoughts
Constantly fighting off other people's haunts
Back in call, always to please, sometimes I wonder
What about my needs, as it begins to hinder?
Do I really exist, left in guilt, I turn and leave?
Don't want to shut them out, it's a mission to please

Yet we come to our end, it's not in my blame
Why should I feel hurt, take in all its shame?
Irresistible was what I once wished for
Never thought to walk through that door
A time has come to focus on what I can
A time has come as no control is what I am

If my spoken words may hit a nerve
As they set the battle, it's how it's served
If it's truth they want, they can take its turn
The defence in lyrics of words that burn
To mimic logistics for power to control
I'll shake you down, it's my power I'm told

Karma is all I enforce, its power strong in mind
I will take in its fear and reverse the time
Bring in your threats, I will haunt you cold
A drive-in hate will mend what's been told
Secrets may carry and will eat you inside
The solider in me will fight for the truth, can't hide

Someday they'll grasp, understand such words
To all that shake as her lyrics are heard
The ones who have no faith, it's just a blur
A rude awaking will come, the wrath emerged
Forgiveness shall beg, the souls may burn
Then when asked the "why," it's Karma learned.

By: Giulia Ricciardi
2006

Resolute

So again, I sit and question my survival
The confusion it's played from our rivals
And only a constant rhythm to express a story
Because it's all we have, it's a simple remedy
It's not for us to believe we're all so perfect
It's just unpredictable, so simple, we deflect
We all foresee it, what we have we've been taught
Acknowledging this is the pretentious thought

Pushed too far from ourselves to enable
Consequences was unexpected, kept stable
Can you turn to humour when it happens?
Does it make you sick to see the signs of caution?
Afraid to fail, you collapse in calling
Left to scream, the expressions fallen
You can look above to seek the answers you need
Perhaps take a moment, reflect thoughts in between

My refuge, my belief can't seem to help me
A bounce in fate has turned against me
Allowing to dwell makes for no solutions
Tears released for a dream in my resolution
Past decisions may have marked me wrong
To fall again, it's just not where I belong
Just to speak can sometimes hurt
Just to love can sometimes make me burn

So, catch that fallen star and make that wish
To have that faith can be our fallen bliss
Undressing these thoughts is all I need
Just to express the reason that may be
I listen to other's lyrics and pray for inspiration
Though it helps the confusion in my aspirations
I can combine my own emotions and lay it out
To resolute, to conquer what I'm writing about.

By: Giulia Ricciardi
April 2007

Crowned

Hidden a burden deep below, I'm drifting away
As the confusion has left me to go astray
It's just what I'm feeling, finding my place
I can feel the frustration it's written on my face
We've had our problems, it's what's to be expected
We are human, part of it can't be perfected

We can push, we pull, get lost in the confusion
Feeling a pain, remember the loss, hide the burden
There is nothing to be ashamed of if you're lost
Everyone has their judgements, it becomes the cost
That feeling of being ripped apart I know too well
It's become my norm, part of my daily hell

As we grow, expectations become a little more
Tougher we become as it encourages that storm
As your world becomes emptier to say the least
Not anticipating battling some demon's beast
We are in this together for you're not alone
My perfect piece of blessing you gave us a home

Shocker, this has become our lives' complete havoc
A few good times in between, memories so classic
Just don't get down and lost, give up that easy
Great things will come to us, this we must believe
You have built me up in my life's worst disasters
You are the one, the key, the crowned master.

By: Giulia Ricciardi

Embraced Friendship by Valor

At times, questions may run through our minds
Exhausted we become a race for time
It escalates in directions beyond our control
For disappointment becomes a haunt in our soul

Unique we become, hiding in vain our true colours
Acceptance always a battle, history inherited its valor
Knowledge is shed, wisdom spared towards us all
As our seed spreads, self protection breaks our wall

So precious yet resilient, a reflection in the mirror
Once was, once had, one's belief all has hero's
A leader, we strive, setting examples to follow
Our instincts may not always agree, it's what we know

Trained and marked has become our given nature
In self acceptance we enhanced our future
You are a light that guides direction unknown
For you've left your mark, a friendship told

Intentions sought out for your all-in heart
A given fact which in fear bears to part
For friendship in play such an importance
Sometimes it may pass without a second glance

Neurotic it must seem, such a mark that's left
Yet unknown to you this I must express
Admiration for the person I see, honour is my valor
For this shall be my mark for the friendship I honour.

By: Giulia Ricciardi

The Dance

Watch your step, wouldn't want you to stumble
Listen for that simple beat, don't be so humble
Take those steps and let your body move
Flow with the melody, let your mind loose
Music can be the reason to make things clear
Find your harmony and dance around your fears

Take a deep breath, envision how it makes you feel
Let it take you to a place where you can become free
I've been many times, to this place filled with melody
It separates the negative to a place of positivity
So, don't look back, forget the judging let's get started
Express yourself, feel the embrace of the warm-hearted

Take away the pain and just go find your way to peace
Spin around, move your feet, find your way to this ecstasy
Don't lose anytime on wasted drama that proceeds
You won't believe how the music fills your veins, it bleeds
It will shake away all that's been given to its despair
Fill you heart with the energy of love with a dash of flair

Reach for the stars, twist your body, take it away my friend
Reach deep down inside, jump the hurdles, create a trend
Take my hand, spin me around, toss me about, catch my fall
Look into my eyes, try not to lose focus, just stand tall
Let's stumble together laugh to all our faults in dance
Again, no judging here it's just me and you in a trance.

By: Giulia Ricciardi

Bitten, I Awoke

The sun will always shine tomorrow, so it's said
Though I've come to terms with my deepest sorrow
Guess I've just wanted to see how it feels
Not realizing I was blinded by its fantasy
I created a world where I thought I was the savior
Again, neglecting my own behavior
I got lost deeper as I drifted
Almost drowning my own existence
But then time took in its effect
When I crossed a path with a poisoned insect
A blurred high is what it gave me
A feeling inside which changed the hatred in me
And like a flash one moment in time
Taunted all my temptations and highs
Broke a spirit I shared deep inside

I became weak and just wanted to unleash
An emotional barrier to release a beast
Pushed away each chance I gave
Just to realize the example I have laid
Allowing the poison to mend what breaks
A bond once strong now left to ache
Two souls became found thought it could help
But that love now sits on a shelf
The comfort in fighting the wrong
Just to be somewhere I belong
There will be a time I get lost again
Next time I will not sit back and pretend
Thought I could stay and embrace the presence
Truth in the matter, it's just an essence
Nevertheless, it's awakened my true being
My greatest wish to conquer its true meaning.

By: Giulia Ricciardi
February 10, 2007

If I

If I could tell you this a thousand times
I could sit here and write 'til I'm blind
But I see so much of a hidden identity
Which blows my mind from the reality?
We all pretend to hide our trust side
Knowing it's wrong, who cares about the ties
Can't be afraid for it's what they want
Tired of feeding into everyone's faults
This is who I am, don't care of the hate
Don't want to hear – you're just a fake
So sick inside, justifying myself
When you're the one asking what I felt
You want the reason, strive for its conclusion
You're at fault, it's your resolution
For what I choose is my decision
Shouldn't be the reason you've become hidden

If I could be your girl, tell me what you think
If it's about you holding back, it's not a good thing
I've been there before, its where you're heading
Can't stop now and just keep me guessing
Just spit it out, if it's about me, just let it go
Don't hold on to me just for show
Can't keep waiting for you, not what I'm about
The essence of time allows me to just bounce
If I take a second look, I know what I want
I'm not here for the show, not here to flaunt
You're the one I want to be a part of me
You're the one I include in my future dreams
If I could be your girl, I'd cherish all my thoughts
If I could be your girl no more secrets left to haunt
I would give you everything, be on top of my being
It would be a blessing, given to what I believe in

If I will stay until the morning shines
If I give you that space, allow the time
If there is a friendship, there waiting to rise
Just don't hold back, it's about that time.

By: Giulia Ricciardi,
April 2007

My Path

You know the ones who like to preach their words
To belittle the ones who seem weak, from what I heard
Don't get me wrong I'm all about freedom of speech
What I don't understand, these ones are like leeches
So, I'm about to strut my stuff, find a new flock
Can't take the shock of it, well let's talk a walk

As I'm going down street side, I tend to walk on by
Looking ahead I see this beautiful sight before my eyes
Nature's beautiful and how it makes me feel inside
As the birds are chirping, the sun shines its rays so bright
But if you can't seem to take the time to see you're tripping
For it won't change my mind, in this world we're slipping

It seems messed up, having to pick the pieces up
Do you understand what I am truly talking about?
Read between the lines, just shake it off, cut it out
Time to move forward no more times left to shout
What are you waiting for? Come on let's go
An adventure awaits down this road, time to show

I'm creating my own path, leaving my trail behind
Come and follow me, we will make it the best of times
It may be rough at times as naysayers along the way
Hey, stand tall, the gods are on our side, a beautiful day
Like the streams that flow to any given destination
We will grab a paddle, move forward with no hesitation.

By: Giulia Ricciardi

Another Crush

Got me vibing, like I just can't resist
Keep me floating along, keep on persisting
Your energy just feeds my body, no time to rest
Like a constant high put it to the test
Let me seduce you, I know you can't resist
Let me hypnotize you to its best

Come on baby doll, I just wanna play
Can you blame this girl, left in disarray?
Just wanna please you until the nights turn to day
Want to mess around, come on boy
I have place in mind, can you stay

I've said it before, got me tripping all the way
Think it's a little childish, well no time for games
I know what you're thinking
I see what you say
How can I convince you?
Just follow my play
I'll let you even lead the way

You're in my sights, speaking of words so strange
Do you get my flow, the words I'm trying to say?
Let's create a new melody,
The beats are pumping, can you hear them play
Can't stop now it's the bed that's laid
Just to seduce you fuels me babe
It torches the fire, listen to what I have to say

Come on baby doll, just hit that note
Play it off, you've got the flow
Start with your fingertips
Work your magic, share your tricks
You've got it going on unleash the beast
I'll play the tease, just more to please
We can start with drinks, relax the room
I'll drink my wine, set the mood
Take off your clothes nothing's new
Move to the beat, let the music move
We've got it started, no stress on time
Tonight, has no limits, you're all but mine.

By: Giulia Ricciardi
May 27, 2007

Follow Me

Baby boy, sometimes you see what you want to see
Sometimes you hear what you want to hear, believe me
Try to understand as I am not one to be deceived
I ask this of you, please have a little faith in me
I can understand, we just seem to analyze (it's what we see)
I can see it becomes to your disguise (to what we believe)
How we have become so blind (a curse it seems)
Unleash what were feeling inside (maybe it's just me)

Baby, just release it, have no time to hate it
Can't think of why we need to judge this
Too much time has come to pass this by
Not trying to complicate it, just give it a try
For no matter what becomes of this, no lies
At least we gave it a shot, doesn't hurt to try

Spin the wheels its been a long road of drama (this I see)
We forget at times that to push past the trauma (this I feel)
Not all the roads are not always paved in gold
Hell, it's the journey of treasures, of our story told
Shake it through your body, you know that negativity
Standing tall we came make it to worlds of possibilities
We can't change the tags that we carry, marked we become
For we let go of our ghosts and journey to a new world, I'm done

Carved and stamped is the package that we carry with us
Let's get lost between a world far and beyond, why the fuss
Create a different tune, just throwing down some thoughts
I want to share my world with you, we can visit the tropics
Tall palm trees, beautiful waters with sandy beaches
Oh, I wish we can close our eyes, escape from this reality
I want to get lost with you, baby doll, why can't you just see
Nothing is perfect in this crazy life, so let's start our own story.

By: Giulia Ricciardi
May 2007

The Player's Side

I have a little story to tell you, which you've heard before
You can't seem to want to hear, would rather close that door
Because for once someone truly believes in you, look no more
Its not about the game or the score, it's what you're looking for
You have battled your demons, you have felt all its pressure
You have sacrificed the distance you have discovered
You've been broken, took a chance, consumed your pleasure
It's about your choices, your decisions, now or never

There is so much about you which scares you inside
You see all the darkness, not what really shines
At one time you could look into my eyes
Now, it like my sight just burns in plain disguise
Towards this story I just wanted you to know
I've come a long way now, it's hard to let you know
I can't fight what I'm feeling, I've fought it before
Yet with everything going on, it may take its toll

Your past is so broken for everyone passed to have seen
Your heart has been blasted, I've heard your words scream
And yes, its been drastic, for the most part it seems
We all what to escape at times, this I can agree
For we all want to erase the times, hell, it's no disguise
Does it really matter, it's the player I recognise?
But I just wanted to let you know what you mean to me
Though I may have some regret, this is hard for me

Sometimes it's just a leap in faith that's needed to help
It can alter any wrong decisions and hurtful regrets
Sometimes our past can create our future behavior
Then try to become the ones to be the saviour
But sometimes we want the rush and go for the ride
Not realizing at times along the way it may hurt inside
For not everyone's path is meant to be followed
I just wanted you to know we all have a past of sorrows.

By: Giulia Ricciardi
April 2007

A Vision in Thought

Woke up this morning with visions flowing around in my head
Thinking of this guy and who has made things come to an end
He would show he cared and then distant he becomes to haunt
He preaches his words, then it absorbs in my thoughts
He set me aside as to him, well, I wasn't his normal per say
And though he isn't even around not sure why it bothers my day
Was I to think that maybe he could have become that one?
Than lo and behold, my mistake, how could I have been so dumb

They seem to hesitate beyond my comparison in thought I see
The truth always shines right through them, so it seems
It has become such a constant challenge these men I find
The pick of the litter is just not a fun game for my time
For it just ends up being another sad story to tell
Of this chaos of love and hurt, my daily piece of hell
Then we all seem to lose that faith, no doubt for reality
To find that one with deep expression a taste for commonality

With boundaries that can be changed and have some balance
These playful hearts that gallop in the night with fun and dance
Just searching for someone that's true and common sense
Oh, the web we weave running about creating unneeded stress
And its not so wrong for these lessons which can be learned
Any thought in doubt, the door left open to leave on my terms
For I may fall at times, become weak, become the dark
At least it's no surprise for when I leave, a given mark

Just looking for excitement in the wrong places, I guess
Looking to have some fun and give my broken heart a rest
The warm embrace when the morning light glimmers and shines
That comfortability lying naked to someone enjoying my time
To have that morning coffee reminiscing about our night
To have some laughs, joke around asking "whatcha doing tonight"
Just seems to be the pick of the litter, these men I find I guess
Maybe down the road my heart will find its match at its best.

By: Giulia Ricciardi

Balancing the Times

Rhythm runs through my veins, becoming electrifying
Rattling the mind, overwhelming me, it's defying
It's first step can sometimes paralyze our surroundings
Which can make us feel barricaded to become grounded
We see what we see, restricted to express ourselves
Conformed and repressed, limited to the request for help

The prize at hand inhibits what we want to gain
The words in lyrics turn the norm to pain
Now who's the prisoner in their own domain connected
For good is bad at times, what's understood is pathetic
All questions are their own opinions suggested
So, who becomes in the right and states commitments?

As I sit back and reminisce of all my little stories
I take a second to embrace the possible glory
This girl who was raised with such consequences
Of the battles listed through her life's given chances
We see our culture through a looking glass of one race
As tradition once set, has now become an open place

We were taught to believe in a given speech
Even through our struggles we kept the peace
For they all knew us, yet keep their distance
As a sickness set upon one, we didn't stand a chance
Yet shunned in a New York minute I felt angered
To find even blood could turn against human nature

The gods were our only blessing, it kept us stronger
As the years passed by I didn't stay around much longer
Strayed away to start new beginnings in a different city
Through hearts were broken I needed to balance my sanity
Though I was not alone had friends to guide me through
My experiences started again with a different view.

By Giulia Ricciardi
May 2007

Ring me a Tune

Got a lot of thoughts in my head, it's ringing
At times I feel a part of me is singing
Trying to analyse what things mean
Trying to give some chance of reasoning
And a lot of times it just gets messed up
A lot of time I felt a loss of control
But then I remember this is my highway
Destination unknown, what more can I say

If this is how it must be, then just let me be
If this is how I am, just try to understand me
Why must I fight to claim my destiny
This is all I got, just set me free
Got a lot of guts, so I've been told
Got a lot of faults so the story goes
Dreams of fortune begin to unfold
Just pieces in my life start to be told

I investigate my life and I come to realize
I'm in the limelight yet don't recognize
Such confusion in me tends to blow me away
This is my time, what more can I say
A little drink on: oops! Not my day
For it's all about peace why the despair
Set back, let go this is my thing
Can you understand the melody that rings?

As the notes may play over in my head
Even laid out, not sure to what is said
But as the wind gusts outside my wall
Doesn't overpower that sound at all
Embellish each pictured thought I see
Only to regress the state of my reality.

By: Giulia Ricciardi
2006

Tripping Over You

Take a minute, just listen cuz, babe I'm trippin' over you
You stay away and yet it falls into play, when I'm hearing from you
Just listen cuz babe I'm trippin', and it's only cuz I'm thinking of you
You have me guessing no questions, no reason
And it's making me crazy over you
I can't breathe at times, when I hear a rhyme
You got me thinking over you
You've become my drug; your words know me so true
But I must just stop thinking of you

You have me, don't fight me, just hear me
Cuz baby it's all because of you
I must be tripping, just hits me, and shakes me
Cuz you have me mesmerized over you
You got me spinning all over, make me think
All over you, just question, because of you
We're not perfect, sometimes stupid, not thinking
And it's all cuz I'm crazy over you

Baby boy, can you hear this song, cuz it's all about only you
You're just the only one to make me sing this song
And it's all because I'm tripping over you
What will it take just to realize, I'm true to you?
I just wanna know why I feel this for you
When we play in notes, sometimes we can be so cruel
You hate to love me, I hate to love you
Love to hate me, love to hate you
So why am I tripping over you?

You get me so excited when I hear your voice
And I'm back to getting stuck over you
You come around in time, with good intentions
A little twisted and so lost left here so confused
Can't make it out, nor play it, got it twisted
And its all over you, why fight it
Just break it, why hide it, just show it
Still keeps me trippin' over you

I just lose control when I think of you
Just get all crazy, a loss of words to spit out a few
Just makes no sense why this comes over me
You're the medicine which cures the disease
Should I fight it, can I stop it, maybe I really like it
My high has become over you

By: Giulia Ricciardi, April 8, 2007

I Hear from You

It's funny at times how you hit me up
Thinking about how you keep me pumped
And it takes you a minute to listen to
I know your heart is just being true
Baby, it's funny how it takes one word
Even far-away talking online makes me move

For I have no worries, I can feel you
I hear you clear, just lost with you
And when I'm hurting, in a worry
It just takes one word and I scurry
I'm no longer stumbling, its true
Cuz it's just when I hear from you

Chorus: You keep me healing, my head is spinning
       And all it took was a listen, who am I kidding
       Just to hear, I have no worries, just need to address
       You have me convinced, no time to stress
       Changed what's become of me, this I find
       How vast things have changed over time
       My days are bright, and this is true
       Cuz it's just when I hear from you

You keep things high above, in check for me
With time you will become the best of me
For now, it's about you and your time to shine
It's what you love, your music, your time
The truth may be no time for fools
It's what I love about you, this is true

It's funny how you make me leap
So much to say when I start to speak
It's hard to see, but it's what I hear
What you mean to me, have no fear
And memories may be short at hand
As I think of you in a far-off land.

By: Giulia Ricciardi
April 2007

Common Mistakes

I heard you had a new girlfriend the other day
And I just lost all the words I had to say
Felt like my heart was broken, yet I knew
Just why it came, how it was the truth
I thought about it, just took my breath away
But I understand just why you had to stay

It seems so hard sometimes, I turn around
Battles cross my path I lose my ground
Just want to escape, it's not the answer I say
I want to admit I strive to achieve each day
I've got my spirit which shines to please
I know each step I take is a mission complete

For I can breathe, no more lost in fear
I can see what's in front of me, I hear
And baby, I know you meant well
I know what you're singing, time will tell
For I am free, you've done me right
Just took the steps to conquer the fight

It took some time to see, some time to feel it
The hurt left inside when you left, I admit
I lost my way, but I now see the light
I've always known on a given night
And yet I've learned from my mistakes
I'm thinking now to let go of the hate

It took so long to get it right, no regrets I say
All in time, yet it feels like it happened yesterday
Looking back at how it played out, accepting my fate
Sometimes it's the cause of common mistakes
Yet I'll miss you, this I can truly say
For now, it's come to be my judgement day.

By: Giulia Ricciardi
2007

Hurting Inside

Each corner I seem to turn, images of you haunt my mind (get away)
Just trying to escape, I'm screaming, hurt inside, (left astray)
All I ever wanted was someone like you (only fate)
Can't seem to shake this feeling away (I pray)
I'm walking alone, and the city streets echo your voice
I'm running down each alley just trying to figure out
What is it that poisons me inside, what is that sound?
Baby, if I could just for a moment, just to hear you say
If I had the chance to say goodbye, I'd ask you to stay

Is it too late to say goodbye?
Is that why it hurts inside
Baby, I find this empty hole
I can't seem to fill its void
I need just to hear you say:
One day girl, one fate girl
Don't give up girl, one love, baby girl
Just give me a little bit of faith
My doll, I'll always keep you safe
It's never too late

The November rain reflects my memories (baby wait)
It's driving down the corner, the melody hits a beat
I'm feeling so alone, just as you left me
I can figure all the reasons why, I'm hurting so
Can't just accept this, please hear me (can't let go)
I can hear your voice whisper pass me (just touch me)
Your picture never erases my mind (I'm crying inside)

The sweetness of your lips
The embrace that keeps me safe
The fact I still believe in fate
Just wanna scream, no more mistakes (I pray)
Just wanna hold you in my arms
Just wanna escape, what will it take
I'm holding on to hope, can't take this no more
I've stripped my disguise
You've seen what I hide
You've kept me alive
You alone are what I recognise

When I close my eyes at night, I pray to the morning lights
Was it all a dream, was I hypnotized?
Like a driving force I put up a fight (just fate)
Like some bull horns I attack (that's just hate)
I'm out of control, just come release me
Before I become out of my mind, don't hate me
For your desired kiss is what I miss
You've left me stripped beyond belief (baby please)
Just don't try to fight me, baby just love me
Tell me you won't forget me
Tell me you will be true to me

By: Giulia Ricciardi
May 26, 2007

Letting Go

For every untold story there is a reason being
Just to hear the drama, the frustration of it leaving
You can lose your mind knowing its lingering there
Take a minute, reflect a bit, absorb it, make it aware
There's always a reason as it's told, to be heard
Allowing it to consume you, well, that's just absurd

It may not make any sense at first, as it may burn
But, in its moment, the obsession is there to learn
What's the point in overthinking all the dramatics?
The who, what, why, will send you in complete hysterics
All that matters is you take a second look, move along
Try some mediation, try to put it in an expressive song

Sometimes writing the words uncovers the expression
Sometimes it's finding the right people to just listen
All wounds need to heal, for this does take some time
Go to that place to lean on, a place you can unwind
Life can be a battle, always someone shutting you down
Just fight it out, find some peaceful common ground

Cut those lingering ties, for you're not here alone
Embark on a new adventure, drop the stones
For, always new adventure starts at square one
At least somewhere new, you've become undone
Don't look back to its end, start your journey
The story has been set, my friend, it's your destiny.

By: Giulia Ricciardi

That Girl

You make me wanna scream and shout, where to start?
It's like a message I've tried to say before, let it part
What the hell they just don't seem to understand
Gotta play it out, I'm thinking, coming up with a plan
Jump in my world for a sec, trying to save them all
Unfortunately, I am that dreamer, waiting to catch my fall

Waiting for you to call me up, that knock on my door I linger
Searching to occupy myself, trying hard not to point that finger
For late nights seem to be the place where I seem to fall
The devil's drink has consumed to what's become my call
Its like poison filling my veins, turning heads helps the game
Shit, too much thinking has distorted me, becoming hard to tame

There's a beast inside wanting to break free, wants to shout
Her suppressed anger rages inside her, please do watch out
Nothing good to become of this estranged being laid
For her image tainted, her emotions twisted, it may fade
To a place where all is normal to her yet quenching a thirst
Here we go again, preaching about her, that given curse

I wouldn't test the waters, though others don't seem to care
Thinking she's just that girl, ya know, the one who tears
Your emotions up and splits you in two from one look
Thinks all psychological, who digs deeps to write her book
But her heart is solid like the gold from the deep I pray tell
This girl who screams and shouts at times with a rage from hell.

By: Giulia Ricciardi

Just an Adventure

Caught up in a bubble here though I'd hate to admit
Sometimes solutions that pass hands turn to shit
I try to step away, control myself, holding back my anger
As I turn to tears afraid of what I just might hunger
I will just make it worse, it will deal itself out
Still young and jaded, that's all I feel that counts

Generations may change, a constant learning curve
Ambitious, always having something to prove
Always around a different scene, just to admit
Sometimes I'm uptight, for this I am just a little bit
Protecting my surroundings, I can't sit in silence
I remove myself from toxic people, break that fence

Then off I go, to another journey that I'm feeling
Down that road again, looking for that next meeting
Maybe this time I can find some salvation deserved
Maybe I'll uncover what I'm about, that learning curve
It's becoming never-ending, these directions that I go
Can't seem to sit still, just bored for this you must know

I can see where I'm stepping on too, make no mistake
What I have learned to value, well that's what's at stake
There's no such thing as fairy tales, I've convinced myself
It's all lies so why play the part, why go looking for help
I just need to pop that bubble and get on with it
Live on to my adventures, aren't you curious, just a bit?

By: Giulia Ricciardi

Live Another Day

You've heard it all before, trying to figure out my past
Despite the challenges I have faced as they seem to last
Beyond such time the pain that hides have now turned to collide
My expectations have been faced to be placed, or pushed aside
There have only been very few who have taken the time to speak
To listen and give sound advice, who understand the fight I seek
For my own blood has no idea or even knows my hidden battles
The mistakes I've made, the shadows haunting my soul, it rattles

I wish they could see how the past has taken its toll, it owns me
Some days I wake up and I just can't breathe, it's choking me
If they could just stop pretending, they know what I'm about
Take a moment of their precious time, lose the sense of doubt
Sometimes a simple hug or the sense of acknowledgement to say
Don't be afraid, move forward and live towards another day
Words of encouragement is just a simple task, I seem to repeat
That dial tone has become the sound I hear when I try to reach

A prisoner I have become in my dwelling, it's breaking my heart
I don't know what I have done, the years have pushed us apart
And each day I awake to a fresh new start, no one by my side
Does make it harder for one to admit, crushes my pride
So much I just wish to confide, the fear of what I might bear
The secrets buried which have scarred me beyond compare
I take a moment, take myself to a place where I can scream
At the top of my lungs, it's the air that I breathe

As toxic as it may be at times, there is relief too when I cry
It sheds that skin, that thick layer of hurt, that web of lies
I've taught myself to withstand this so-called circle of trust
I'm growing each day to realize changes have become a must
I know the future ahead may hold more battles to conquer
It may take some time, but I'm sure I'll rise from that bunker
My family will always be there, the timing isn't right for today
At least I have my writing, I can survive, I'll live another day.

By: Giulia Ricciardi
April 2007

A Dream

If I gave you a melody could you make it dance
Could you make it beat, leave me in a trance?
Could you give it harmony, come on give it a try?
Blow off some steam, dance our worries of life
Our everyday may learn to withhold some havoc
Allow the music to silence that constant static

It binds the need, helps us carry on, sets aside the worry
It brings me to a place where the sun shines, birds chirping
The waters run clean amongst the rocks, trickling down
The wild runs free for nature's beauty is its only crowd
A blessed sound that becomes so hypnotizing to my ears
Thoughts are peaceful and carried away, have no fear

You share the passion as you allow your body to groove
You absorb its light above by setting your own mood
The ground only rumbles beneath when the bass kicks in
By then you're left mesmerized as nature has sucked you in
You spin round and round, no care for which direction
You soul has become lifted by glory with no rejections

As the sun begins to sink, slowly setting its rays to rest
Winding down is the only thing that becomes the test
That feeling of euphoria is running through your veins
Not quite ready to settle as the music pours like rain
Beyond the distance I see a place like a sea of meadows
I scurry on finding another place, like hills of pillows

The night is catching on, the moons shines to the fullest
It brightens up the skies as the music is at its best
Fireflies start to glimmer surrounding as back ground lights
Crickets are harmonizing in the grass below calming the night
As the melody starts to slowly come towards its end, I see
I awake to the sound of my fire crackling right beside me.

By: Giulia Ricciardi

The Secret Garden

Painted clouds hover in the sky
The moon is full and the only source of light
Voices chanting and whispering: Nature's cry
The winds are cool all through the night
Drip, Drip the water goes off the leaves of the tall palm trees
Sounds of waves crashing in the distance
As the shivers start to crawl through your body
You're beginning to fall into a trance
Your eyes start to feel heavy as you collapse to the ground
Visions painted slowly, there are no bounds
As you come to a deep sleep, tainted pictures are all you see
No reason to escape as there's no way out
A mission set as your surroundings build up
Lights flashing, sounds of whispers start chanting
"Move with me, come and you'll see a place where life was meant to be."
You're getting weaker as it pulls you closer
No chance trying to fight it, for its power is much stronger
The lights get brighter the whispers get louder
Before you know it, everything has become still
Your eyes begin to open slowly, the vison start to fulfill
As you grasp at your surroundings, your mind is calm
Embrace the beauty as the morning dawn
The skies start to move behind the tall mountains
Fresh flowers bloom by the fresh water fountain
As you think to yourself, this is where I'd rather be
Away from the chaos of all life's negativity
I move towards the fields of green, running towards this peaceful scene
Dancing and spinning no cares in mind
Embracing nature's beauty, protected and kind
The hands of time start to tick, the sounds get louder
You know it's become that time no sense to wonder
The clouds start to hover, as your body begins to shiver
Drip, drip goes the raindrops
Will I return for this? You hope
As nature's cry calls you back once again
You're falling back into a deep sleep once again
As it starts to pull you further away
You know one day your fate will return you someday

For now, the lights draw dim and the whispers fade
Back to its reality as your story has just begun
No time to waste, you open your eyes as it's been fun
Time is moving for what you have discovered
A place called the Secret Garden you have uncovered
And though you know one day you shall return
Your time has spent more knowledge to earn
This different world of peace and harmony
Nature's best kept secret and all its beauty
When it's time, Nature's cry will be heard once again
For then you'll know its time go, let go of the pain
The Secret Garden is where your fate will lie
And all will unveil your peace you will find
With the help of the hands of time
And someday you shall make your way there
This is where your heart will stay, this is where your fate shall bear.

By: Giulia Ricciardi
July 28, 1993

CPSIA information can be obtained
at www.ICGtesting.com
Printed in the USA
LVHW040148151119
637426LV00001B/34